The Witwer Files

D.L. Dennis

The Witwer Files

ISBN-13: 978-1-937089-95-5

Truth Book Publishers
Franklin, IL
www.truthbookpublishers.com

Cover design by Laurel Berkel

Seventh Printing

Printed in the United States of America.

Contents

Acknowledgments		*7*
Introduction		*9*
Chapter 1	Leaving Missouri	13
Chapter 2	Firstborn Brother of the Witwer Clan—Charlie	17
Chapter 3	Jim, the Woodsman	25
Chapter 4	Ernest, the Quiet One	29
Chapter 5	Dick, the Renegade	33
Chapter 6	Early Morning Departure	36
Chapter 7	The Final Good-byes	41
Chapter 8	The Final Chore	47
Chapter 9	The Adventure Begins	50
Chapter 10	A Way of Life	53
Chapter 11	The Day of Destiny	56
Chapter 12	A Fateful Decision	67
Chapter 13	The Official Offer	69
Chapter 14	Hillview	73
Chapter 15	Moving to Hillview	77
Chapter 16	The Hillview Jail	87
Chapter 17	The Ringleaders	93

Chapter 18	Mrs. Greene's Restaurant	96
Chapter 19	The Handbills	101
Chapter 20	Christmas Back Home in Missouri	107
Chapter 21	The Family Gathering	109
Chapter 22	Slick's Demise	115
Chapter 23	The Investigation	126
Chapter 24	The Birth of Everett Eugene	130
Chapter 25	Good-bye, Everett Eugene	139
Chapter 26	October Harassment	149
Chapter 27	An Unusual Offer	153
Chapter 28	Gunshots!	157
Chapter 29	Christmas Eve, 1914	161
Chapter 30	The Calm before the Storm	166
Chapter 31	The Challenge: March 5, 1915	174
Chapter 32	A Bad Omen: March 6, 1915	180
Chapter 33	Kill or Be Killed: March 6, 1915	185
Chapter 34	Call for Support	190
Chapter 35	The Standoff	194
Chapter 36	Sheriff Edwards	198
Chapter 37	The Lockdown	204
Chapter 38	The Flight from Hillview	207
Chapter 39	Witwer Brothers Depart Hillview	212
Chapter 40	A Village Divided	215

Chapter 41	A Charge of Murder!	217
Chapter 42	Jail Time	220
Chapter 43	The Formal Complaint	222
Chapter 44	Life in the County Jail	226
Chapter 45	The Grand Jury	231
Chapter 46	The Trial Begins	235
Chapter 47	Witnesses Are Called	240
Chapter 48	The Verdict	246
Chapter 49	Starting Over	255

Epilogue *257*

Acknowledgments

The four years of research and the writing of *The Witwer Files* has given me the opportunity to be in contact with several individuals who are direct descendants of the Witwer brothers. These individuals related to me stories that have been handed down through their families about the period of time the Witwer brothers were in Hillview, Illinois and the events that took place. It was fascinating to listen to their stories and to be able to share memories with them. Their assistance was invaluable, and I thank each of them for spending time with me.

Catherine (Witwer) Eveleigh, a Witwer historian, graciously provided me with an enormous amount of information she acquired about the Witwer family through her genealogical research.

Joy Witwer, the son of Jim Witwer, provided me with photographs and historical data.

Flo (Witwer) Lowe, the daughter of Dick Witwer, provided me with photographs and stories about her father.

Elmer Witwer (deceased), the son of Ernest Witwer, who lived near where the events in the book took place, provided me with a unique perspective on the characters in the book.

Norman Witwer (deceased), the son of Dick Witwer provided me with numerous stories about the people and events and why some of them happened.

On my first of many trips to Hillview, I had the good fortune to meet Doreen Wear, who has become a friend. She took the time to acquaint me with some of the locations in Hillview, Illinois where the events of this book took place. She told me about the history of Hillview, and helped bring to life all of the stories I had been told. Doreen has provided many of the photographs, which are in the book. I will be forever grateful for her help and her friendship.

I spent many hours walking the streets of Hillview and studying the pictures to visualize the events that took place. While doing research in the Greene County Courthouse and Carrollton Library, the people I encountered enthusiastically assisted me in finding documentation and transcripts necessary to complete the story. My heartfelt thanks to all of them.

D. L. "Don" Dennis
don@donspin.com

Introduction

The Witwer Files is a story but one that was inspired but actual events. The story of Hillview's village marshal, Charlie Witwer, and his deputies happened almost a century ago. In writing this book, I have attempted to provide the reader with as many facts as I could find during my research.

I lived with Charlie and Lucy Witwer, my grandparents, from the time I was six months old and was told many stories by Lucy. I had the opportunity to spend time around Charlie's brothers throughout my youth. The language I have used in this writing, I believe, is consistent with what I remember from their conversations and with the research I have done. This research included interviews with the children of Jim, Ernest, and Dick Witwer. Several of their sons and daughters spent numerous hours with me discussing their fathers, providing me with pictures, genealogy material, and stories about the Hillview shooting that had been passed down in their families. I will be forever grateful for the time they spent with me, not only for their stories and information, but also for giving me even more memories.

While doing this research, I also had the opportunity to meet many people who now live in Hillview and the surrounding area. I spent numerous hours in Hillview walking around the streets, eating at the local cafe, and visiting in people's homes. Many of these people provided me with information and stories that had been told to them about the years my grandfather was the village marshal. I cannot begin to thank them for the time and consideration they gave me. They are wonderful people who love Hillview!

I have taken the liberty of using material found in my research, which includes newspaper articles, court records, genealogy information found in libraries, and conversations with family members and others who had stories to tell about the Hillview shooting, to develop a story line which would make interesting reading. The reader is asked to be aware that I have presented the story of the Witwer brothers and Hillview based on research, but I have taken the liberty to add conversation and events.

On the night of the shooting of Clarence Deeds, the witnesses saw the same event, but there were many different versions told by those witnesses. Stories about Marshal Charlie and his brothers have been handed down from generation to generation. As these stories have been repeated verbally, they may have been changed somewhat but the core elements remained the same. I have made every attempt to put this book together using as much factual information as I could find in my research and have also used the stories told to me by family members and acquaintances familiar with Hillview and its history.

The Witwer Files

by D. L. Dennis

TRUTH BOOK PUBLISHERS

Model T

Charlie at age 18

CHAPTER 1

Leaving Missouri

The year was 1913 in Mexico, a small Missouri town. The warm days of fall had been quick to slide into days that displayed the first hint of what promised to be a long, cold winter. It was a crisp November morning with thick frost that glistened on the rooftops and on the patches of grass in the yard. The frost was so thick the low-lying areas looked like they were covered with crystals and jewels when the sun broke through the scattered clouds and started rising over the horizon. Today the sun would send its warmth to the earth and melt the frost quickly, but everyone felt it was going to be a cold winter.

The four Witwer brothers, Charlie, Jim, Ernest, and Dick, were loading their Model T Ford Touring car early that morning. Jim was the self-appointed "mechanic," so the Model T had been filled with gas and oil the day before. He had checked the car over thoroughly and declared it ready for the trip the brothers were getting ready to embark upon. In the early morning twilight, the only sound to be heard was the dry, brown leaves crunching under their feet as each of the brothers walked briskly from the porch to the car and back to the porch again. With each trip, they grabbed another box or two that had been stacked on the porch waiting to be packed in the car. The car had to be packed carefully to leave room for each of them to have a seat. It was a good thing that none of them was big men so they could squeeze between the boxes.

The Model T was beginning to look rather comical as they piled the boxes high, trying to tie them together to keep them from bouncing around. Their personal belongings were rather meager, but they were stuffing in as many household supplies as they could carry. Of course, each had made sure he had loaded his hunting gear first because hunting season in Illinois, as in Missouri, was about to begin. At least one of the brothers hunted every day during hunting season with the goal of providing meat for the evening meal.

As they made their treks back and forth, one and then another of the brothers stopped for a moment to look around at their neighbors' houses one last time. There was little conversation, as they each were lost in their own thoughts about what life had been like in Mexico. They had lived in Mexico for the past several years, and the days, months, and years had fallen into a familiar pattern. Even though they were excited about the move and their new jobs, leaving behind a life they were familiar with was causing a few pangs of anxiety, although they would never want anyone to suspect it. Each of them was leaving behind loved ones and good friends. They knew they had to put those thoughts behind them. Even though there may have been a twinge or two of uncertainty surfacing in their thoughts that early morning, each of them had made his decision, and they were ready to get that car loaded and be on their way.

Charlie, the oldest of the Witwer brothers, watched his three brothers and knew their thoughts. He had watched his brothers grow into adulthood and knew them well. Once the decision to leave Mexico had been made, Charlie was not one to look back on his decision. He had not coerced his brothers into going with him, but he was glad they were. He had wanted each of them to make his own decision to leave and did not want to influence them. They were leaving their hometown of Mexico and were heading to Hillview, Illinois, because Charlie had been appointed to the position of village marshal. His brothers were going to be his deputies. It was not going to be easy for any of them to leave, but the decisions had been made.

Hillview, whose population was about 630, was situated on the Illinois River and was one of the fastest growing communities in Illinois. It was a farming community with rich, fertile ground in the fields. Even though it was a small community, it had been experiencing an unusually large number of troublesome problems, most of which were created by gangs of young men roaming the streets and drinking too much. These troublemakers were often referred to as "river rats." Most of them were well known in the community, with one or two of them being from prominent families. The village was desperate for a marshal who would restore peace and order. An offer had been made to Charlie to fill that position. Without a village marshal, the troublemakers were taking advantage of the situation.

This offer to Charlie had come about through some very unusual circumstances. One of the conditions of accepting the position that Charlie had insisted on was that he could appoint his own deputies. The Mayor of Hillview had assured Charlie that he could appoint whomever he wanted as his deputies. Having this authority was an important factor that Charlie's decision to take the position hinged on. He knew he had no desire to take on the challenge of being the village marshal unless his brothers would be his deputies. Once Charlie told his brothers about the offer and asked them if they wanted to be his deputies, it had not taken long for the three brothers to agree to be deputies, even though it meant moving from Mexico.

These four brothers had spent a lot of time together throughout the years. Their lives were so entwined that it was hard for any of them to imagine not being together. There were two other sons born into the Witwer family. Frank was born in May of 1890 and no longer lived in Mexico. He had moved to Springfield, Illinois, to marry a young woman by the name of Ethel Kennett. Harry was a young boy of sixteen when his older brothers decided to make the move to Hillview. Harry was a studious lad and did not spend much time with his older brothers.

Charlie's decision to consider taking the position as village marshal was understandable since he had some experience in law enforcement, but the decisions of his brothers had nothing to do with experience or qualifications. Being a deputy would certainly be a new adventure, but the excitement of a new adventure was only part of the answer. Each one of them had his own personal reason for uprooting and leaving his hometown of Mexico.

Jim and Ernest each had wives, and they were more than happy to have an excuse to leave Mexico. Ernest was also leaving a child behind, but that fact did not slow him down in making his decision. This was not something Jim or Ernest talked about openly, but anyone who knew them could figure it out. Dick had the least realistic idea of what it was all about, but he was the most excited about being a deputy with his big brother, Charlie. To Dick, the move and being a deputy was just another adventure in life. He had always been a tag-along no matter what Charlie did, so it was no different this time. Whatever Charlie did, Dick tagged along.

Charlie was the oldest, and the three brothers had always looked up to him. As they grew up, they had been close as brothers and liked being together, so it was not a difficult decision for any of them to make, regardless of what they were leaving behind.

CHAPTER 2

Firstborn Brother of the Witwer Clan—Charlie

Charles R. Witwer was born on February 18, 1882, on Island 55 in the middle of the Mississippi River. Even though he was born on this island, his birth certificate showed Callaway County, Missouri. There was no middle name given, just the initial, something Charlie would ponder on from time to time. A short time after Charlie's birth, his parents moved to a small farming community, where his father took whatever job was available so he could provide for his family. There was not a lot of money, but there was always food on the table. As the oldest male in the family, Charlie accepted whatever responsibilities his parents expected him to shoulder. As with many families during those years, schooling was not a priority. After attending the local one-room schoolhouse for a couple of years, Charlie spent little time in school and a lot of time with his dad. He learned early in his life how to be independent and how to help take care of his little brothers as they came into the family.

Charlie enjoyed several years of single life before marrying Lucille Claywell, affectionately known to everyone as Lucy. He was thirty-one when he and Lucy tied the knot. Charlie's Cherokee Indian blood, inherited from his mother's side of the family, was reflected in his appearance—jet-black hair, dark eyes, and a prominent nose. He was considered to be quite a handsome man by the ladies. Charlie was not a man of many words, nor did his emotions surface often, so with those who did not know him well, he developed a reputation for being somewhat aloof. Those who knew him, though, saw the warmth of his personality and knew he was someone to be depended on as a reliable friend.

As he grew into adolescence, Charlie spent much of his free time in the woods hunting, trapping, and logging. While spending time with his father, he learned some of the skills his father used to support the family. He learned how to work with horses, which helped him get work as a young man. He spent his days working for some of the local farmers and helping with the family garden, but the woods was his favorite place to be.

Charlie never shied away from the girls in his teen years, but as he grew into early adulthood, he began to fancy himself as quite a ladies' man. When Saturday afternoon came, it was time to put the hunting gear away, get rid of the horse smell, and get ready for a Saturday night dance. The first thing in order was to take his bath in the old, battered galvanized tub filled with water from the cistern that had been heated on the wood stove. Whatever house the family lived in always had an enclosed back porch with curtains strung across a wire on the glass windows. That is where the old tub was set. When the door to this back porch was closed, everyone else in the family knew that someone was taking a bath and to stay out. The weekly bath was something everyone in the family enjoyed, and no one wanted to be disturbed, but Charlie was a real stickler. He did not want anybody bothering him, and you just might be yelled at if you did. After getting cleaned up, Charlie would then head to the local barbershop for a shave and maybe a haircut. Charlie was very vain about his appearance and tried to make sure that none of the other men, young or old, around town looked any neater or was better dressed than he was, particularly on Saturday night.

After the trip to the barbershop, Charlie would head back to the house. You would not find many "Sunday meetin'" clothes in his closet, but he always had a good suit or two for Saturday nights. Once he was back home, he would pull his best suit out of the closet, brush it off, and polish his boots to a high sheen. He took great care as he donned that suit and those boots, but he was only fully dressed once he got his hat on. Then he was ready for a night out on the town. The neighbors would see him strutting down the street, and they knew he was headed to a dance. Charlie was a good dancer and had no trouble in finding a dance partner—all of the girls wanted to dance with him. He had no trouble in attracting the ladies—young or old. He would flirt with them, court them, but never gave any of them a reason to think he was looking for a serious relationship. He played the field throughout his twenties, which gave the local women a lot to talk about. Who was going to be the one that would finally catch Charlie?

Charlie's younger brother Dick usually tagged along with him to the dances. They would head to a square dance in their hometown or go to one of the neighboring towns, if they thought that was where the most girls would be. Much to Charlie's chagrin, he spent much of his time trying to keep Dick out of trouble instead of dancing. Charlie was not much of a drinker, but Dick did his fair share, even though he was barely out of his teens. Quite often, Charlie would have to drag Dick away from the dance hall just to keep him from getting into a fight. When this happened, you could bet that Dick got an earful the next day, but that did not stop him from tagging along the next weekend.

It was at one of those Saturday night dances in Mexico that Charlie and Dick met two very attractive sisters, Lucy and Liz Claywell. Lucy was not quite seventeen years old, and Liz was just fifteen but tagged along with her older sister every chance she got. Charlie was smitten with Lucy as soon as he met her, and Dick took a fancy to Liz. Charlie remembered seeing Lucy walk into the dance in a lace-trimmed, yellow-flowered dress. He watched her as she and Liz walked over to a group of young ladies, and his heart skipped a beat. Charlie thought Lucy was the prettiest one in the bunch! It did not take very long before he started courting Lucy every weekend. He had been a bachelor for many years, but Charlie fell fast and hard for Lucy.

Lucy's parents strenuously objected to her being courted by Charlie, and they certainly did not want Dick hanging around Liz. First, they knew Charlie was thirteen years older than Lucy and that he ran around with an older crowd. They did not want Lucy involved with a crowd that was so much older than she was. In addition, the Witwer brothers certainly did not have sterling reputations, particularly Dick. This courtship caused a lot of tension in the Claywell household. As each weekend approached, the arguments would start about whether Lucy and Liz could go to the dance if Charlie and Dick came around. It was bad enough to have one Witwer brother coming around to court one of their daughters, but they had two of them. Lucy thought Charlie was quite a catch, so when she turned eighteen, she told her parents in no uncertain terms that she intended to marry Charlie Witwer—and she did just that.

Charlie had always enjoyed being single, flirting with all of the girls at the dances, and doing what he wanted to do in his spare time. By this time in his life, he had a good job, and he had avoided thinking much about matrimony, until he met Lucy. Meeting Lucy was the beginning of the end of Charlie's single life! Much to the surprise of everyone, once he started courting Lucy in spite of her parent's objections, Charlie did not have time for other girls. Lucy was determined to marry Charlie, so she did everything she could to make sure he spent his free time with her.

During their courtship days, Charlie worked as a railroad detective on the Kansas City–Chicago Railroad.

The railroad allowed him free passage to any destination within their system. Lucy had hardly ever been outside of the county and dreamed about seeing the "big city," Chicago. She told Charlie she would marry him if he would take her to the big city, but Charlie did not have any desire to go to Chicago. As the courtship evolved, though, his desire to marry Lucy overtook his desire for the single life. Once Lucy made that declaration, it did not take Charlie long to take the leap into marriage even if it meant he would have to take her to Chicago. He and Lucy spent their honeymoon in Chicago after being married by a justice of peace in Chicago on June 29, 1913.

Much to Lucy's dismay, it was a very short honeymoon. It was not the exciting trip to see the sites in the big city that she was expecting. Charlie thought that spending a few days in Chicago would be a small price to pay to get Lucy to marry him but after he was there for a couple of days, he was ready to leave and get back to Mexico. His description of Chicago was "streets full o' horse shit and ya couldn't walk anywhere without gittin' in it." So back to Mexico they went to begin their married life. Lucy moved from her parents' home into the Witwer household, which included Charlie's parents and brothers Harry and Dick.

Charlie knew that life as a married man would bring about some major changes in his life, but little did he know that life was soon going to change even more than he had anticipated. Within a few weeks after returning to Mexico from the honeymoon, Lucy decided it was time to tell Charlie the news. By that time, she was sure she was pregnant. She needed to tell Charlie that he was going to be a father! Charlie was far from being ecstatic about this news but accepted the situation. He had never been a person to shirk his responsibilities, and this sure was not the time to start. He had wanted to marry Lucy, and now he was going to be a father also. Of course, once Lucy told Charlie and her family, the news spread very rapidly and was the "talk of the town" for several weeks.

Lucy did not like Charlie working as a railroad detective because he worked long hours. Even though she was not alone in the house and her family was close by, she missed Charlie. She wanted him to be home more. She quite often told Charlie about her feelings, and told him she wanted him to quit working for the railroad and find other work. Charlie disagreed with her, which caused some very heated discussions between the two of them. The rest of the family would scatter when these discussions were taking place. Both of them were good at standing their ground and their stubbornness would surface. Charlie tried to make Lucy understand that he was making good money, and now that there was a baby coming, he needed a good paying job. He did not have much luck in convincing Lucy, though, and this was a dark cloud hanging over the two newlyweds.

Charlie knew he had only two years of formal education and felt he was lucky to have the job with the railroad. A few months later, when he was offered the job as the village marshal in Hillview, being a detective with the railroad played a part in him being offered that position. The experience he had gained on the railroad also gave him the confidence to accept the challenge.

Lucy at age 18

Jim, the woodsman

CHAPTER 3

Jim, the Woodsman

The next Witwer brother born was James "Jim" Wiley Witwer on May 20, 1884. Jim did not look like his brother Charlie but resembled his father, Jacob, whose ancestors were German and Swiss. Even though Jim was a stocky man, his ability to move quickly amazed his friends—and many times his foes. If backed into a corner, he oftentimes would be the first one to throw a punch, and many times that was the only punch thrown. He did not often start a fight, but he did not back down from one either.

Jim was generally thought to be rather withdrawn and quiet, to the point that many of the townsfolk thought he was a shy fellow. Some said he talked more to his hunting dogs than he did to people. Jim loved his hunting dogs and was content spending time hunting wolves or whatever was in season to be hunted. He also spent time trapping fur-bearing animals so he could sell the hides to earn money. These activities were common among the men, both young and old, that lived in small rural towns. Jim did not view his dogs as just animals with which to hunt. He truly loved those dogs! If Jim could buy, sell, or trade a hunting dog, it would be the highpoint of his day. Oftentimes he would be so attached to one or two of his dogs that he hated to replace them when they lost their usefulness in the timber.

Like Charlie, Jim had little formal education. Until he married, Jim lived with his parents and Charlie doing various jobs he could pick up to help with the household expenses. Life was never very exciting in their small town, so he quite often would frequent the dances with Charlie.

When Jim was twenty-three, he married Hattie Spencer, which turned out to be an unfortunate match from the beginning of the "I dos." Jim and Hattie set up their own household rather than living with either of their parents. To say that their life together was less than ideal was not a good description. It was a very unhappy union almost from the very beginning. Jim did not shy away from work, but he tried not to let it get in the way of his hunting and trapping, so between hunting, trapping, and working, he was gone much of the time. This was not Hattie's definition of a marriage.

Since Charlie was still single in those early years of Jim's marriage, Charlie could spend his free time as he wished. Once the newness of marriage had worn off, which was not more than a few weeks, Jim wanted to run around once again with Charlie. Charlie and tag-along little brother Dick were going to the dances on Saturday nights and chasing the girls. So, within a short time, not only did Jim spend his free time hunting and trapping, but he also left on Saturday nights with Charlie and Dick to go to the dances, and he did not take Hattie.

Jim followed his big brother's footsteps and liked to get dressed up on Saturday nights. He was known for always sporting a vest under his suit coat and wearing black high top, lace-up shoes. When Jim started getting cleaned up on Saturday afternoon and headed to the local barbershop, Hattie knew what his plans were. That is when the bickering would start. It was not uncommon to get the old washtub out for a Saturday bath, but when Jim headed out the door to the barbershop, Hattie knew that it meant another Saturday night alone. The minute Jim got home she would be standing at the door with a scowl on her face, ready to pick a fight. When the windows were open on warmer days, the neighbors could hear the rise and fall of the words being thrown back and forth.

Little brother Dick was hardly old enough to be chasing girls, but Hattie knew that he tagged along after Charlie, and the two of them did not go to the dances just to dance. Hattie had been to plenty of dances, and she knew they were flirting and chasing as many young ladies as they could. She did not want Jim to be with them but wanted him to be with her. Rarely did Hattie convince Jim to stay home, nor did she convince him to take her to the dance.

Ernest and Bertha (second wife), shortly after their wedding

CHAPTER 4

Ernest, the Quiet One

Ernest Witwer, the third of the brothers born into the Witwer family, was born on March 20 of 1886. Like Charlie, Ernest had the Cherokee Indian blood characteristics—coal black, straight hair with dark brown eyes, and the prominent nose. There were now three boys in the Witwer household, each about two years apart. Life was the same for Ernest as it was for Charlie and Jim as the years passed. Going to school was not a priority, and he went to work with his dad as often as he could, particularly when his dad was working on someone's farm. His perfect day was to be able to spend it on a farm roaming through the cornfields and checking out the horses and cows. His brothers would tease him when he came home, telling him he smelled like the cows, or something worse! That did not bother Ernest one bit. Charlie and Jim had their hunting, and he had his farms.

As Ernest grew to be a young man, he began dreaming of owning his own farm. He had grown to love farm life and wanted to raise cattle and grow corn and wheat, but too many circumstances in life got in the way of his dreams. One of the detours was his marriage to Sadie Spicer. This marriage was clouded by some very unusual circumstances.

Ernest and Sadie began keeping company when he was about twenty years old. Sadie gave birth to a baby boy, Glenn, in July of 1906. She named Ernest as the father on the birth certificate even though they were not married at the time of the birth. This certainly gave the gossipers something to pass around when they picked up their mail or ate at the local restaurant. Neither during the pregnancy nor at the time of the baby's birth did Ernest intend to marry Sadie. As the months passed, Sadie and her family tried to coerce Ernest into marrying Sadie. Ernest eventually folded under the pressure and gave up his freedom. All of the Witwer brothers valued their freedom and did not give it up easily. Ernest and Sadie were united in marriage in April of 1907 when Glenn was nine months old.

To add even more confusion to the situation and cause more gossip, on the birth certificate, Glenn's name was listed as Glenn Whitworth, not Glenn Witwer. It was common for young ladies to be illiterate, but compounding the situation, Sadie had a speech impediment and did not speak very clearly. When the doctor asked for the father's name, he understood Sadie to say "Whitworth" rather than "Witwer," so Glenn was forever to be known as Glenn Whitworth. Ernest always regretted succumbing to the pressure to marry Sadie. When the opportunity presented itself to leave Mexico and go with Charlie, Ernest was more than happy to have an excuse to leave—and he had no intention of taking Sadie and the child with him.

Dick, the renegade

CHAPTER 5

Dick, the Renegade

Cecil Witwer, who during his youth became known as Dick, was born on May 27, 1892, six years after Ernest. Dick was a scrawny kid who was often in trouble. He was always trying to keep up with his older brothers. Dick attended school off and on, more off than on. He tagged along after Charlie as much as Charlie would tolerate him.

On Dick's fifteenth birthday, Charlie gave him a single-shot 4/10 shotgun with a pistol grip. It was called a boot gun because it had a short 12-inch barrel. Many times the owner would hide the gun in one of his boots. When the gun was shot, it had a kickback like a mule but it was not very accurate.

Dick was very proud of his new shotgun and, like any fifteen-year-old would do, was showing it off to some of the older boys in town one afternoon. One of them laughed at him and said, "You couldn't hit me in the ass with that thing if you tried."

Throwing a challenge like that out to a Witwer was just not the thing to do, especially not to fifteen-year-old Dick who was always out to prove himself. Dick quickly responded, "If ya put yer ass up, we'll see if I can hit it."

The fellow turned around, bent over, and Dick proceeded to shoot him in the rear. Fortunately, the fellow had on heavy overalls, and the 4/10 shotgun had number eight birdshot in the load. The fellow did require some minor medical attention, but at least he was still alive. It did not turn out to be a serious injury, but Dick had to suffer the consequences for taking on that challenge.

As the events of the day unfolded, someone called the local police, and Dick was arrested. He was turned over to the juvenile authorities and was brought before a circuit judge in Mexico. He pleaded his case before the judge, telling him, "I was just tryin' ta scare the guy. I didn't think the gun was loaded."

Dick's reputation as a troublemaker and as a young lad who skipped more days of school than what he attended was well known in the community. If he had not been in so many skirmishes before, the judge may have been more lenient on him. That was not the case. The judge sentenced Dick to two years in the Booneville Boys Reformatory in Booneville, Missouri.

Dick's behavior did not change in the reformatory, and his performance was less than stellar. He spent more than his share of time in detention. After the story was circulated among the other boys in the reformatory of why Dick was there, he got the nickname of Buckshot. All it took was one of the other boys to call him Buckshot, and Dick would start swinging. The fists would fly, which would result in another detention. Twice, he and one of the other boys tried to run away. Of course, he was caught and each time his sentence was extended. Dick was not one to learn very quickly from his mistakes.

While Dick was in the reformatory, he did acquire some basic math skills and rudimentary reading skills, but the most impressive skill he learned was how to operate a sewing machine and also how to repair one. This turned out to be a most valuable skill in his adult life.

With detention after detention being added to the two-year sentence, Dick was finally able to walk through the gates to freedom after about three years in the Booneville Boys Reformatory. Dick was released into the custody of his oldest brother, Charlie, and forever left behind the nickname of Buckshot. At least, no one ever called him Buckshot to his face! Charlie always had misgivings about giving Dick that shotgun but hoped that maybe these three years in the reformatory would have taken some of the wildness out of Dick. Charlie took Dick back to Mexico to live with him and their parents, but it did not take Charlie long to realize that those years did little to take the spitfire out of Dick.

Charlie knew that the best thing for Dick was to make him get a job so he would not have much spare time. Charlie hoped that would keep him out of trouble. Dick spent the next couple of years working at A. P. Green Brickyard and making a dollar wherever he could. Dick was like his brothers in that he did not shy away from working, but he did not like the brickyard. Much to Charlie's chagrin, once again Dick followed Charlie to the dances on Saturday nights. He was older now, but he was still the irritating little brother to Charlie. Dick continued to be a renegade but managed to stay on the right side of the law.

Dick met Lucy's sister, Liz, at one of the dances and took a liking to her. Liz was only fifteen, though, and her parents forbid her to see Dick. Dick was not the kind of fellow they wanted courting their daughter. To Liz, Dick's past just added to the excitement of having an older boy interested in her. Liz would slip away on Saturday nights and go to the dances with her sister, Lucy. Dick was not ready to be tied down with a wife, so in those early months he was content with their courtship being limited to when he saw Liz at the dances. A little spark flared up every time he saw her, though, and Liz could see it in his eyes. She hoped that it would just be a matter of time until he took a serious look at her, and she eventually got her wish

CHAPTER 6

Early Morning Departure

The loaded 1910 Model T Ford Touring car, crammed with as many boxes as it could hold with a couple tied down on the running board, sat in the early morning shadows beckoning the four brothers. Jim, Ernest, and Dick wanted be on their way without any more delay, but they did not want to seem too anxious to the rest of the family. The anticipation and preparation for leaving made each of them a little jittery. They knew Liz and Lucy were cooking breakfast, but the brothers were so anxious to get on the road, they were just about ready to grab a hot biscuit and be on their way. Not one of them said a word, but each kept darting looks at Charlie, who seemed to be making a point of ignoring them as he walked around the car checking this box and that box.

The Model T seemed to be sinking further into the ruts in the yard as it was loaded with the boxes. The car was usually parked in the front yard since they did not have a driveway. With the fall rains, the ruts in the yard became deeper and deeper each time it was driven in and out of the yard. Even though the morning air was nippy and ice crystals where gleaming on what little grass there was, it had not been cold enough to make the ruts turn into frozen tracks. Not many of their neighbors could afford a car, so the brothers were proud to have their car sitting in the front yard, regardless of how many ruts were made. Only a couple of the brothers could drive, but each of them had chipped in to buy the old Model T, so each of them was proud to claim ownership.

Model T automobiles had no starters and had to be cranked by hand to get the engine running. Many fellows broke their thumbs while turning the crank of a Model T. The Model T did not have a heater, and the only protection against the sharp winter wind and rain was treated oilcloths attached to the overhead frame of the vehicle. A roof was made by pulling the frame and oilcloth from the back over the top and then attaching it to the windshield frame. This roof provided some protection over the heads of those riding in the car. The side curtains, also made of treated oilcloth, were pulled down and hooked to the tops of the doors. These side curtains gave the driver and the passengers a little protection from blowing wind and rain and from mud splashing in as they traveled the muddy roads. Traveling any distance in cold weather required warm clothing, gloves, and a cap with earflaps. Even then, journeys were not pleasant in the winter months, but it sure was better than traveling in a wagon pulled by horses or worse yet, on horseback.

It was not long before Lucy rapped on the windowpane in the front door and motioned for them to come into the house. As the door was opened, the smells floating through the air made them realize that taking time for breakfast was a good idea. Their stomachs growled and their mouths watered just at the thought of what had been cooked in those iron skillets. Lucy, Charlie's wife, and her younger sister Liz, who lived only a few houses away with her parents, had gotten up very early to fix platters of eggs, bacon, and biscuits for all of them to have before the brothers took off on their day’s journey. Lucy insisted on frying two skillets full of chicken and making extra biscuits so a dinner could be packed for the brothers to have as they made their trip.

Before daylight, when Jacob and Nancy heard the clattering of skillets in the kitchen and Lucy giving Liz orders, they knew it was time to get up. Breakfast would be ready soon, and they wanted to be with their boys on their day of departure to bid them farewell. The house—the homestead—in which they all lived belonged to Jacob and Nancy. Charlie and Dick had not moved out of the family home as they grew into adulthood. When Charlie married, he brought his bride, Lucy, back to the homestead to be a part of the household. Lucy had taken over much of the cooking, which was just fine with Nancy. She had spent many years cooking and cleaning for those men folk, so she was ready to sit back and take it easy.

The house was not a fancy house, nor was it in one of the better neighborhoods, but it was the family home, full of memories for all of them. The faded paint was peeling off the wooden porch railings, the old plaster in the kitchen was cracked, the flowered wallpaper was peeling in most of the rooms, and the floors creaked every time a step was taken, but it was their home. Most of the houses on the street looked just the same—faded, peeling paint, bare yards, and dog pens in the backyards, along with rusted clothesline poles. Most of them were occupied by more than one generation, and quite often, there would be little ones playing in the yards and running up and down the sidewalks.

Platters of food were sitting on the stove to stay warm. As the four brothers came into the kitchen, Liz poured everyone a hot cup of coffee from the old, blue-speckled, enameled coffeepot. The cups were stained from the hundreds of cups of coffee that had been poured into them, and a chip or two could be seen on the handles. Charlie, Dick, Jacob, and Nancy sat in their usual spots, while Ernest and Jim each grabbed a chair from the corner of the kitchen and dragged them up to the table. After setting the steaming platters of eggs, bacon, gravy, and biscuits on the table, Lucy took her apron off and sat down by Charlie. Liz took her chair and squeezed in beside Dick. Harry stood quietly in the kitchen doorway wondering where he was going to squeeze a chair in. Nancy motioned for him to get a chair and sit by her.

As the platters were passed around and everyone began to eat, there was very little conversation. The silence was deafening. The only sound was the scraping of a fork on a plate or a spoon hitting the side of the coffee cup. When someone wanted the jar of the homemade jam or the bowl of butter, they just reached across the table rather than ask for it to be passed. It seemed as though everyone had lost his or her ability to speak.

All of their faces were bent toward their plates as they scooped the food onto their forks and into their mouths. No one wanted any of the others to see whatever emotion was playing on his or her face, whether it was sadness or anticipation of a new adventure. The brothers were anxious to be on the road even though they each felt sadness about leaving.

Neither Lucy nor Liz could swallow a bite. The big lumps in their throats just sat there no matter how many times they tried to swallow and make them go away. They knew that even the grease-covered eggs would not slide down past those lumps. They picked at their food and pushed it around their plates. No one noticed, since each person was lost in his or her own little world.

Thoughts were flying around in Lucy's head as she wondered when Charlie would send for her. Liz wondered if she would ever see Dick again, or if he was going to leave and forget her. Jacob and Nancy were sad to see all of them leaving at once. There had always been at least one of the older boys living with them, so to have them all gone was going to leave an empty spot. Nancy knew she still had Harry at home but he was growing up fast.

Jim, gobbling his food down, was the first one to finish. He swallowed the last of his coffee, shoved his chair back and bolted out of the door without saying a word or looking at anyone. The other three brothers ate in silence until there was not a crumb left on their plates. Breakfast had always been a main meal in the Witwer household, and Lucy and Liz outdid themselves that morning. The brothers knew Lucy was packing a dinner for them, but after that was gone, they were not sure when their next good, hot meal would be. They were not looking forward to cooking for themselves. They probably would have to find the local diner to get a good meal. It was not long before the only sound was the scraping of chair legs as Charlie, Dick, and Ernest pushed their chairs away from the table. As they made their way to the door, Lucy, Liz, Jacob, Nancy, and Harry looked up with sad eyes brimming with tears.

CHAPTER 7

The Final Good-Byes

Lucy and Liz stood shivering on the front porch with the tails of their thin, cotton housedresses rippling in the breeze as it blew across the porch, while Harry, Jacob and Nancy stood back in the doorway. A feeling of sadness hung in the air as the five stood watching the activity in the yard. They avoided looking at each other for fear that their emotions would erupt. This strange turn of events, which started with the job offer to Charlie, was unsettling to those who were being left behind. When Charlie first came home with the story of what had taken place on their trip to buy and sell hunting dogs, no one could have imagined that it would lead to what was happening that morning—four leaving and five standing in the early morning light, watching and knowing they were being left behind. No one had asked Jim about his wife, Hattie, nor did anyone ask Ernest about his wife, Sadie, or baby Glenn. Jim and Ernest had made it clear that they were going to Hillview—alone!

Memories flashed through the minds of Jacob and Nancy as they watched their four boys preparing to leave. Ernest and Jim did not live with them but were never far away. Not many days would go by before one or the other of them would end up at their kitchen table for a meal. Charlie had always lived with them, and Dick might be gone a night or two, but they always knew he would be back. Even though both of them were sad to see their boys leave, they were glad the four would be staying together. Family was an important part of their lives.

Anticipation of what was to come flooded the minds of Lucy and Liz as they wrapped their arms around themselves trying to keep warm. Except for an occasional shiver that ran through their bodies, they both stood so still they looked like two statues. Lucy was lost in thought as to what her life was going to be like once Charlie left, and then her mind jumped ahead to when she would join him in Hillview. She was anxious for him to come back for her, yet she could not envision leaving her family, friends, and all that was familiar to her. She hoped Charlie would come back for her before their baby was born, though. She had grown to care for Harry, Jacob and Nancy in the short months she lived with them, but she knew that nothing was going to make up for Charlie being gone. She wanted desperately to go with him, but knew that it just was not possible. Charlie was only going to be about sixty miles away, but to her, he might as well have been six thousand miles.

Liz only had eyes for Dick. She wondered if he was going to come back for her or forget her when he left town. Thoughts of Dick finding another girl ran rampant through her mind. She tried to block out the visions of him dancing with other girls at the Saturday night dances as they floated through her mind. She knew Charlie would not be going to dances now that he was married to Lucy, but she was sure nothing would keep Dick home on a Saturday night. Liz knew her parents were happy that Dick was leaving and would pester her to go out with some of the other fellows. She had already made up her mind that she was not going to listen to them. She just did not want to go out with other fellows. Even if her parents thought Dick was a rascal, she was going to wait for him to come back for her.

As they stood watching and waiting, it was difficult for Lucy to hold back the sobs that were making it difficult for her to swallow. Her chest felt like it had an anvil sitting on top of it. Thoughts flew threw her mind of what had taken place in just a few short months. She was only nineteen years old and pregnant. She and Charlie had not been married but a few months, and she was just becoming adjusted to living with Charlie's family. Now Charlie was not going to be there at all! She was confident that Charlie would come back for her. She knew she would be reluctant to say good-bye to her family and friends in Mexico, but she just wanted to be with Charlie. She did not know what the future had in store for them, but she was anxious to know what was going to happen next. Where would they live? How was she going to live with four men? Who was going to be with her when their baby is born? All of these thoughts were running around in her head, and her bottom lip quivered but not from the cold air. Her eyes were glassed over with tears that had not yet spilled over to run down her cheeks.

As the brothers looked at what was still stacked on the porch, they decided they just might have to leave a few things behind. They had to leave enough room so each of them had a place to sit. None of the brothers had many personal belongings, but they wanted to take most of what they had. Charlie had an extra box packed with his good wool suit and an extra pair of highly polished black boots. When he was packing them, Lucy told him, "Don't ya be goin' ta any dances wearin' that suit an' them boots." Charlie did not have that in mind when he was packing them, but he did not want to leave them behind.

Hats were important, and each brother had at least one felt dress hat or a Western-style wide-brimmed hat. A man's hat was as much a part of his attire as was his shirt, pants, and boots, and they were not going to be left behind. After shoving boxes around and doing a lot of grunting, Charlie decided the old Model T could not hold anymore, and they were ready to go. A couple of battered suitcases were tied down to the large running boards, so they had to climb over them to get in. While packing their belongings in the car, one thing they made sure of was to leave room for their guns—shotguns and rifles that were used for hunting—and plenty of ammunition.

TIMBER WOLVES were once a menace to stock in this area, and a bounty was offered on them. This photo, taken September 7, 1929, at the Morgan County Court House, shows a group of men with some wolves which had just been killed on the Cliff Davis farm between Pisgah and Orleans. Shown holding the dogs, left to right, are Jim Witwer, Dick Witwer, Bert Allen [illegible]. A few of the others who could be identified include Denby Ranson, Floyd Allen, John Defrates, Dr. Albyn Wolfe, Leavitt Arnold, Richard Arnold and George L. Riggs, then serving as Morgan County treasurer.

Final chore, loading the dogs

CHAPTER 8

The Final Chore

The last chore to be done before they were to be on their way was to hook the homemade dog pen onto the back of the car. Jim had spent many hours making that dog pen, and he was proud of it. It had woven wire sides hooked onto a wooden floor with a gate across the back. As Jim dragged the pen around to the front of the house, the dogs penned up in the backyard started barking and yelping. Jim yelled at them to be quiet so they would not wake up the rest of the neighborhood. It was hard to tell who was going to wake up the neighbors first—the ruckus the dogs were making or Jim yelling at the dogs!

The dogs had been loaded into that pen many times to go on hunting trips, so they sensed something was going to happen when they saw Jim moving the pen. They did not know there would be no hunting trip today, but instead they would be taking a long ride. After Jim got the dog pen hooked onto the back bumper, he went to the backyard and opened the gate to let the dogs run loose. Those three dogs tore around to the front yard, yapping all the way. The dog pen gate was open, and the three dogs jumped up into it before Jim could get back around the house.

These dogs were as important as the shotguns and rifles that had been loaded into the car. Timber wolves were plentiful in Illinois and Missouri, and the dogs were trained to track wolves. A generous bounty was paid to hunters for every wolf hide that was taken in. Occasionally, one of the dogs had to fight a wolf that had been cornered, and sometimes the dog came out on the short end. When that happened, the dog ran whining back to its master with a piece of his ear gone or some other injury.

There was nothing pretty about these three dogs, but Jim loved them anyway. Each one was a mixed breed with scars and tattered ears. One of them had even lost an eye in a battle with one of the timber wolves he had cornered. This old hound still had a lot of fight left in him, and there was no way Jim was going to leave him behind. It was quite common for hunting dogs to fight among themselves, but the two younger dogs were wise enough to leave "Old One Eye" alone. He was definitely the alpha dog. Each of the Witwer brothers had done his share of hunting with the dogs, but Jim was their master. Jim loved to hunt, and those dogs were his partners.

After everything was loaded and the dog pen was securely tied onto the car, it suddenly got very quiet—even the dogs quit barking. No one said a word for a few seconds. They all looked at the ground or pretended to be fiddling with something, wondering who was going to make the first move to say good-bye. They tried to avoid looking at one another, hoping that it did not have to be them. Everyone knew the final good-byes had to be said, but who was going to be first?

Impulsive Dick could not take it any longer. He was the first one to make a move as he jumped up on the porch, grabbed Liz by the shoulders, and kissed her on the cheek. This broke the electrifying tension that was flowing among them. Not one to show much emotion, Jacob offered his hand to each one of his sons, but Nancy grabbed each one and gave them a big hug. Charlie took Lucy's arm and guided her back into the house. Charlie, like his father, was not an emotional man and did not want to say that final good-bye to Lucy in front of everyone.

Once all of the good-byes were said, hugs given and tears shed, the brothers could not hide the excitement they felt. They were anxious to be on their way. Jacob, Nancy, Harry, Lucy, and Liz stood on the warped steps of the house as Charlie, Dick, and Ernest made their way to the car. Jim crouched in front of it and began turning the crank. After a few cranks without the engine catching, Jim began to cuss and mumbled under his breath, “Somebody oughta shoot Henry Ford.”

Finally, after a few more cranks, like a stubborn Missouri mule, the Model T began to make its familiar rhythmic putt-putt sound. Jim jumped into the driver’s seat while Ernest and Dick hopped into the cramped seats in the back. Charlie climbed into the front passenger seat, and as Jim started slowly rolling out of the yard, Charlie's stoic face broke into a brief smile as he looked at Lucy and said, “Pack yer suitcase, hon. I’ll be back soon.” Everyone waved as the car rolled out of the yard through the ruts and onto the street. The Witwer brothers were headed to a new challenge in Hillview, Illinois.

CHAPTER 9

The Adventure Begins

As they rolled out of town, it was too early to see many other cars on the street. As a few wagons passed by, the horses would whinny and shy away from the car. Not many words passed between the brothers as they took one last look at the town they called home. They drove down the rutted, gravel street with anticipation of what was to come. Charlie was thinking about Lucy and knew he would be back as soon as he could to get her, but the other three brothers were only thinking about getting to Hillview. They were looking forward to their new adventure. After Jim had been driving for about an hour and mulling things over, he looked over at Charlie with a frown on his face and said, "What the hell did we git ourselves into? Yer the only one who knows anythin' 'bout law enforcement, an' I'm not too sure that ya know that much. Bein' a marshal in Hillview 'r any other place is a hell of a lot different than ya bein' a railroad detective. An' we're supposed ta be yer deputies! We ain't never been deputies!"

Charlie's eyes flashed with anger as he looked around at his brothers. He looked at each one of them, and they could tell by the red stain that appeared on his cheeks that he was mad. He glared at Jim as he said, "If any of ya don't want ta be my deputies, we'll just stop the car right now. Ya can git out an' walk back ta Mexico 'r hitch a ride with the next car 'r wagon that comes along." Jim hunched his shoulders over the steering wheel and kept his eyes on the road, not daring to say another word. When Charlie's cheeks turned red, Jim knew it was time to keep his mouth shut.

Dick, who was sitting behind Charlie in the backseat, piped up and said, "Bein' a deputy in Hillview cain't be any worse'n the years I spent in the reformatory in Booneville 'r workin' in that brickyard. I hated that place." Silence fell on the brothers as they continued to drive in an easterly direction toward Louisiana, Missouri, where the ferry would take them across the Mississippi River to the Illinois side. Even though the sun was beginning to shine brightly, the cold air seeped in around the windshield. An occasional shiver from the cold air ran through their bodies as they bumped along the rutted road, wishing the trip was over. They had not seen another car on the road, but it was still early in the day. They passed several wagons being pulled by teams of horses, and everyone waved as they passed. Even though they were cold, at least they were traveling faster than the wagons. They passed by cow pastures, small country houses, and cornfields with nothing in them but the stubble left from the harvest.

Charlie was not paying much attention to what they were passing as his thoughts were on Lucy and the baby she was carrying. He looked at his brothers and wondered what was going through their minds. Even though he had not tried to influence their decisions, he felt a sense of responsibility toward them. Were they glad they were leaving everything behind? Were they having second thoughts? None of them was very good at talking about their feelings. He finally broke the silence and said, "As soon as we git the house that I rented set up, I'm goin' ta bring Lucy over here. If ya want ta bring yer wives, we'll bring 'em too."

Dick, who was not married, was the first one to jump in with a response. "I want ta bring Liz over here if she'll marry me. She better not take up with that Mann fella before I git back ta git her. When he found out I was leavin' town, he's been hangin' 'round too much. Can ya believe everybody calls him Sugar Cookie? With a nickname like that, I don't know why any girl would want 'im hangin' 'round." They all looked at Dick in amazement. They knew he was sweet on Liz, but they had never heard him talk about marrying her. None of them could picture Dick settled down with a wife!

Jim, who was trying to avoid the potholes as he drove along the gravel road, glanced over at Charlie and said, "I've had all I kin take of bein' married to Hattie. I sure ain't bringin' her ta Hillview. I ain't leavin' my dogs behind, but I sure kin leave her behind. I'd rather git shot bein' a deputy than ta have ta live with her anymore."

Ernest frowned as he said, "I'm damn well goin' ta stay with ya, Charlie. I ain't bringin' Sadie an' that kid ta Hillview."

Charlie did not particularly like what he was hearing, but it did not surprise him. He had thought that a good part of the reason Jim and Ernest had agreed so readily to leave Mexico and become deputies was that they wanted to get as far away from their wives as they could. Neither had said anything to him, but it was not hard for Charlie to figure it out. The Witwer brothers were leaving three wives behind, one who was pregnant and another one with a child. One brother was leaving his sweetheart behind. On one hand, Charlie was grateful to his brothers for agreeing to be his deputies, but on the other, he felt a shade of remorse thinking about the two wives and child being left behind. They would not become part of the family in Hillview.

Chapter 10

A Way of Life

At the turn of the century, the average wage in a small Midwestern town was about twenty cents an hour. As each of the Witwer boys got old enough to work, it was expected that they would bring home some of their earnings each week to help support the family. They cut railroad ties and white oak timber, which was sold to be made into whiskey barrels. At an early age, Jacob had taught each of them to use a broad ax and a crosscut saw. There was little thought given to making them attend school to get an education, and none of the boys objected. After a long, hard day in the timber, each of them would make about two dollars a day. A good part of those earnings was used to help support their parents and the family home, but some was kept in their pockets for spending money. Their mother, Nancy, had a mason jar in the pantry for them to put their contribution in. She knew when payday was, kept close track of how much was in that jar, and how much was added to it.

Charlie, Jim, and Dick liked to spend their extra money on Saturday night courting clothes so they could be well dressed when they courted the girls. Jim tried to squirrel away a few coins away in a secret hiding place. He just might run across another hunting dog he wanted to buy. Ernest always seemed to have a little extra money in his pocket. He was not into buying hunting dogs or courting clothes, so if he had any left over after providing for Sadie and Glenn, he tried to keep it. He still had that dream of owning a farm. Dick was always broke. It was as if he had a hole in his pocket. He always tried to borrow money from Ernest when he ran short. Ernest knew Dick would never pay him back, so he tried to avoid him when he thought Dick was coming around to borrow money.

As each one of the brothers grew into their teen years, working long hard hours was expected in the Witwer family, and it was not something to be argued about. Jacob never shied away from work, and he did not accept any excuses from his boys. Work began at sunup and did not end until the sun was set. In their teen years, they were rather scrawny and did not look like they could do a hard day's work, but they were a scrappy bunch. Even in adulthood, not one of them grew to be over 5'8", nor did any of them weigh more than 150 pounds.

The work they did was not easy, and the pay they received was usually based on how productive they were. What they took home at the end of the day would depend on how many railroad ties they were able to cut or how many logs were cut to be made into barrels or lumber. After the timber was cut, it then had to be dragged out of the woods behind a team of horses or mules. The work was physically demanding and dangerous. If anyone was hit by a falling tree or slashed with a broad ax, it often meant the loss of a life since the nearest medical help was miles away.

In addition to working in the timber, the Witwer brothers learned to plow the ground with a team of horses, which they did for farmers and neighbors. They also trapped wild game to sell the pelts. They hunted rabbits and squirrels as much as possible to take home for their dinner table. Charlie had a way with horses and was often asked to break a horse so it could be ridden or used with a team for pulling a plow or wagon.

Like most families in small rural towns, their daily lives were determined by the cycle of the seasons—spring was plowing, summer was working in the timber, fall was harvesting, and winter was hunting and trapping. It was a way of life for the Witwer brothers, as it was for most of the families in their neighborhood. Charlie was the oldest and was a good worker, setting an example while Jim and Ernest followed. Dick was another matter. None of the Witwers ever backed down from a fight, but trouble always seemed to find Dick even though he was a good worker. Dick was like a magnet for trouble.

CHAPTER 11

The Day of Destiny

As the Model T putted and bumped along the gravel road, backfiring occasionally, Charlie's thoughts drifted back in time a few months to the chain of events that had taken place that led to his being hired as the village marshal of Hillview. He recalled the day that he, Jim, Ernest, and Dick were driving down this same road. Jim had heard there were hunting dogs for sale or trade across the river near White Hall, Illinois. The three of them decided to go with Jim to check it out, so they tied the dog pen on the back of the Model T, put the dogs in their pen, and jumped in the car. Jim could never pass up the opportunity to buy or sell a hunting dog. If he bought a new one, or traded one, he would love the new one just as much as the one he traded. Jim just loved hunting dogs. He had a natural instinct for training dogs and always got premium dollars for his hunting dogs. Charlie remembered that it had been a Saturday, and they were looking forward to having the day off. They figured they would have some fun, and it might even be a profitable trip.

After crossing the Illinois River at Pearl, Illinois, Dick, who was barely out of his teens, was itching to find some place to have a drink. The top on the car was down, and even though the wind ruffled his hair as they drove along, he was hot and thirsty. There was not a cloud in the vibrant blue sky, and the golden sun was beating down on them. Dick poked Charlie on the shoulder and told him he was ready for a drink.

Charlie, who always sat in the front passenger seat, turned and said, "It's early. Ya don't need a drink right now. Ya just had dinner a little while ago. After we see 'bout these dogs, maybe we'll drive into Hillview, and maybe we'll stop then. We'll probably all be ready fer a drink by then. It's hot today, and this sun's gittin' ta me." That was not exactly what Dick wanted to hear, but he knew he would not get anywhere arguing with Charlie.

Late in the afternoon, after Jim had taken care of the business with the dogs, they took the gravel road west from Whitehall and headed to Hillview. Dick was the first one to spot the outskirts of the town, and he certainly had not forgotten about having that drink. As they made the last bend in the gravel road, Dick piped up again.

"Charlie, you said we could stop fer a drink, an' I'm dyin' o' thirst."

"I'm sure yer not goin' ta do any dyin', but we'll stop when we git ta Hillview. Just keep quiet 'til we git there."

As they rolled into the main street of Hillview, Charlie spotted a large elm tree across the street from the Phoenix Hotel. There was a large area of shade to park the car and dog pen. He told Jim to pull over under the tree so the car and dog pen would be in the shade. Charlie knew there had to be a saloon close by. Every small town had a saloon or two on the main street.

As they piled out of the car and began stretching their legs, Dick was the first one to spot the saloon a couple of doors from the hotel. He headed straight for it without waiting for the others. Charlie and Ernest followed Dick toward the hotel while Jim checked on the dogs and gave them some bones to keep them quiet. Once that was done, he caught up with Charlie and Ernest and saw that Dick was already pushing the door open to the saloon.

As Dick pushed the heavy wooden door open, he hesitated, letting his eyes adjust to the darkness in the room. The first thing he saw was a long bar with a brass foot rail and spittoons on the floor. This was a familiar site to Dick, as he liked to frequent the saloons every chance he had. As his brothers walked up behind him, the foggy mirror behind the bar reflected their images back at them. The musty smell of stale beer and smoke hung in the air, and the old tin ceiling looked like it had layers of dirt, grime, and smoke caked on it. Not even the fans hanging from the ceiling with their slow moving blades could take the smell out.

Toward the rear of the saloon was a large, black potbellied coal-and-wood-burning stove. A coal bucket and a small scoop used to remove the ashes sat on the floor beside it. The only thing resembling a latrine inside was a small room behind the two card tables in the back where the men stood and relieved themselves. There was a drain hole in the floor, but from what the floor looked like, that drain hole needed to be a lot bigger.

Women did not frequent the saloon, so that drain hole worked just fine even if the boards did have some yellow stain on them. If the fellows in the bar needed any more than that backroom latrine, they either had to go to the old outhouse behind Greene's Restaurant or go to the hotel. The owners of the hotel did not like fellows from the saloon coming over to use the toilet, so most of them used the outhouse. If they went home, they might lose their chair at the card table, or their wife might tell them to stay home. They could not risk either of those, so the old outhouse was just fine. All Dick cared about as he stood in the doorway of the saloon was that the bartender would give him a drink.

After getting their drinks, the four brothers stood lined up at the bar talking about the hunting dogs sitting in the pen outside under the tree and the trade Jim had made that afternoon. There were not many other men in the saloon, and they paid little attention to Charlie and his brothers when they walked in. A few men stood at each end of the bar, some conversing and some just nursing their drinks. You could hear the slap of cards that came from the corner of the saloon where a couple of groups of men were engrossed in a game of poker. Regardless of the time of day or night, there was usually a card game going on.

As if the locals in the saloon knew what was about to take place, all of a sudden all heads turned toward the door. They could hear a ruckus outside as the heavy saloon door was pushed open. The Witwer brothers did not turn to see what the noise was all about but looked in the mirror in front of them. As the saloon door swung open, they could see the silhouettes of four young men bursting through the door, talking loudly, pushing and shoving each other.

As the four young men filled the doorway, they stopped and looked around. A hush immediately fell over the room, and no one made a move. The locals in the saloon were well acquainted with these four young men, or thugs, as they were sometimes described by the townspeople. These four thugs had quite a reputation, and it was not a particularly good one. They, along with several other fellows, had been harassing the townspeople for months, and no one, not even the village marshals, had been able to do anything about it.

Neither Charlie nor his brothers paid much attention to the four as they stood in the doorway murmuring among themselves. One of the thugs swaggered up to the bar and stood behind Charlie.

"Where you guys from?"

Charlie turned around and casually replied, "We're from Missouri. Jus' passin' through. Thought we'd stop fer a drink. Nice town ya got here."

One of the other thugs, standing in the doorway, raised his voice to make sure everyone heard. "We don't like Missourians here, so you better git the hell outta here—right now!"

Charlie was not looking for any trouble and replied with a slight edge in his voice, "We'll be leavin' soon as we finish our drinks."

"You better leave now or we'll throw yer asses outta here."

Not being one to back down to much of anything or anyone, Charlie replied, "That might be harder'n ya think."

At this point, the only sound was the whirring of the fan blades. Nobody moved and nobody made a sound.

It looked like there could be trouble, so Charlie slowly moved his hand to his cane that was lying on the bar. Charlie's always carried his cane with him. He slowly slid his hand to get a good grip on the handle. As he casually turned around, leaning his back against the bar, hooking one of the heels of his boot on the bar rail, he let his arm hang down by his side with his cane in hand. One of the thugs came at Charlie with his fists doubled up. Within a split second, he got close enough to take a swing at Charlie's head. Charlie tightened his grip on the cane and swung it, landing a well-placed blow to the side of the thug's shoulder. As the thug staggered backward, Charlie used his cane to shove him backward across the floor. With all eyes on Charlie, no one had noticed that Dick had quietly skirted around everyone to the door and pushed it open. Charlie pushed the thug through the door and outside. It looked like a well-orchestrated dance with Charlie being in the lead.

Stunned at what had happened so quickly to their friend, the other three thugs turned around and bolted out of the door with Ernest, Jim, and Dick right behind them. Everyone jumped up from the tables, and those at the bar left their drinks. They all exploded into the street to see what was going to happen next.

A few of the local townspeople were milling about on the sidewalks, and a crowd gathered quickly as the eight men scuffled in the street. The townspeople knew who the four thugs were but had never seen the other four. Fists flew through the air and clouds of dust were kicked up as they rolled around in the street. It soon became apparent that the local thugs were no match for the Witwer brothers. They had picked a fight they were not going to win!

The Witwer brothers were not very big in stature, but they knew how to take care of themselves. Years of timberwork had made them strong, and few men ever won a fight, especially when Charlie put his cane to use. After a few minutes, the ringleader had been knocked to his knees. He yelled at his friends to clear out. As he was getting to his feet, Charlie yelled, "How do ya like Missourians now, ya bastard?"

Charlie stood in the middle of the street holding his cane firmly in hand, waiting for one of the thugs to make another move toward him. They had not seen a cane like the one Charlie carried, nor did they have any way to know just how proficient Charlie was with his cane. They certainly had gotten a taste of the damage it could do. As the ringleader staggered to his feet, he looked around at the crowd, recognizing many of the townsfolk. He did not like them to see someone get the best of him. He was used to terrorizing them! After a few cuss words, he nodded to his bruised and bloodied buddies to follow him. Glaring at Charlie as they backed away, they turned and stumbled down the street toward the west end of town.

Charlie looked around at his brothers and said, "Let's go back in an' finish our drinks."

As an afterthought, Charlie said, "Maybe we should make it quick so we don't git arrested fer disturbin' the peace."

It did not take Dick long to dust himself off and head back into the saloon. Jim and Ernest followed along with Charlie, dusting their pants off as they walked along. The men who had been in the bar followed, along with a few of the townspeople who had watched the scuffle. There was a buzz of conversation with everyone wondering who these four strangers were but no one approached the brothers. The local men had never seen anyone stand up to the thugs, and they sure had never seen anyone get the best of them.

Everyone ambled back into the saloon and went back to where they were before the ruckus started. Dick grabbed his glass, drained it quickly, and started mumbling about the hole that had been ripped in the knee of his pants during the scuffle. Jim just grinned and said, "If ya hadn't let that guy knock ya down, ya wouldn't have a hole in yer pant leg. The way yer drinkin', did you git dust in yer mouth?" Dick scowled at Jim and turned away. He just wanted another drink.

Charlie could hear the buzz of conversation as he stood at the bar but nobody approached them. As they finished their drinks and started to pay for them, the bartender walked down behind the bar to where Charlie was standing.

"I'm the owner of this place, and I appreciate you takin' the ruckus to the streets. There'll be no charge for your drinks today. Hope you fellers come back to see us again sometime. Those ruffians cause us a lot of trouble in this here town. You're welcome in my place anytime."

Before Charlie had a chance to respond, the saloon door swung open. Every head turned toward it to see the mayor of Hillview, Lee Coates. Mayor Coates had been in the Phoenix Hotel, and as he came through the lobby, he had seen the crowd of townspeople in the street as the fight was beginning to break up. He saw many of the men go back into the saloon, and saw the four ruffians stumbling down the street in the opposite direction. He knew who those ruffians were and was not surprised to see them in the middle of trouble, but he wondered who the other fellows were. To get to the bottom of what was going on, he figured he should head to the saloon to get some answers.

There was no village marshal to call on for help. He was happy the scuffle did not last any longer than it did, and that apparently no one had been seriously injured.

As Mayor Coates pushed open the door of the saloon, he saw Charlie and his brothers standing at the bar looking like they were getting ready to leave. As he took a few steps toward the bar, Charlie whirled around, tightened his grip on his cane and said, "Stop right there, 'cause if yer a friend of those bastards we just kicked the shit outta, I got some left fer ya."

Mayor Coates threw both hands in the air and replied, "I'm not one of them. I'm the mayor of Hillview. I know who those fellers are, and I know they're usually causing trouble. I saw a crowd in the street as I was walking through the Phoenix Hotel, so I thought I would come over and find out what was going on."

Charlie took a good look at the mayor and said, "We're just tryin' ta have a drink, an' those bastards, whoever they are, tried ta give us some trouble. In most towns, when a fight breaks out, somebody calls the law. How come nobody 'round here called the law? Do ya just let those thugs go around tryin' ta scare people?"

"Sorry this happened to you fellas, but right now, we don't have any law people in Hillview. Somebody threatened to kill our last village marshal and his deputy, and they turned in their badges. They said they didn't want no part of gittin' killed. Before that, we had a village marshal who just disappeared. Never did know what happened to him. I think you can see that we have a problem in Hillview. It's gotten so bad that these ruffians and gangs have got the townspeople so scared, they're almost afraid to come out of their houses. Those ruffians do just about whatever they want, whenever they want. We haven't had any luck in getting anybody to take the job as village marshal since our last one turned in his badge."

Jim, Ernest, and Dick did not say a word, but Charlie knew they were thinking the same thing he was thinking.

"They didn't seem too tough ta me. I'm a railroad detective, an' I deal with ruffians like that all the time. These here 're my brothers. We don't go lookin' fer trouble but we ain't afraid of it."

When the mayor heard this, the thought flashed through his mind that maybe he had found someone who would be willing to be the next village marshal. The village was in desperate need of a marshal, and Charlie and his brothers were the first ones he had seen that had not backed down from the town ruffians. With experience as a railroad detective, this man just might be the right person to take over the job.

Mayor Coates looked at Charlie and said, "Do you have time to sit over here at this table with me for a few minutes?" As Charlie sat down with the mayor, the other three brothers turned back to the bar and ordered another drink.

After Charlie sat down, Mayor Coates said, "You seem to know how to handle yourself. I don't know anything about you, but we need a village marshal. If you checked out to be who you say you are, would you be interested in discussin' the job as our village marshal? Of course, you might need some deputies. We got pretty much of a mess here in Hillview, and we need somebody that's not afraid to clean up the trouble."

Charlie was more than a little surprised and rather skeptical about the mayor's offer, but it aroused his curiosity. As he glanced around the saloon, several thoughts raced through his mind. The first thing he thought about was that Lucy did not like that he was gone as much as he was being a railroad detective, particularly since she was pregnant. He knew he had a good job but figured it did not hurt to talk to the mayor.

"I never thought about leavin' my job, but I just might think 'bout it. That is, if the pays decent, an' if I could chose my own deputies. It looks like I might need more'n one with all the trouble ya say you've had."

"Well," Mayor Coates replied, "Hillview has 250 dollars a month in the budget for law enforcement. The marshal has to pay his own deputies out of that money. Who did you have in mind for your deputies?"

Charlie looked over his shoulder at his three brothers standing a few feet away.

"Those are my brothers. If they kin be my deputies, I just might consider takin' the job. I said 'might.' I'd have ta know more 'bout your town an' 'bout the job."

Mayor Coates looked at the three brothers and said, "That's fine. We just need to sit down and talk things over. Of course, we would have to see if we can get you bonded, but I suppose that won't be a problem since you're a railroad detective."

"I don't think it'd be a problem. Would ya have ta bond my deputies?" Charlie knew that since his brother Dick had spent time in the Booneville Juvenile Correction Center, it might be a problem.

"No, we don't have to bond them."

Charlie turned to look at his brothers, who were standing at the bar as they talked among themselves. He was sure they had heard most of the conversation between himself and Mayor Coates. As he glanced into the mirror and saw their reflections and the expressions on their faces, he knew he needed to talk things over with them. Their brows were furrowed with frowns, and they were acting as if they were ready to head to the car.

Mayor Coates continued the conversation, "I need a little information on your background as a railroad detective and some personal information that I can take to the village council meeting. We have a meeting tonight. We need a marshal so bad I would appoint you right now, but I have to review your credentials with them and get their vote. They all know we need to get somebody in here quick to help us clean up this town."

"There ain't much ta tell. I'm thirty-one years old, married, an' my wife's back in Mexico, Missouri. She's pregnant so I'm goin' ta be a dad 'fore long. Ain't never been in jail, 'cept ta put somebody there. Ain't got much schoolin' but I got a good job. Don't think the railroad would've hired me if I didn't check out."

Jim could hear the dogs barking, so he looked over at Charlie and said, "The dogs are raisin' Cain in their pen out there. We need ta git a move on it."

Charlie turned to the mayor and said, "Looks like we need ta be leavin'. Ya talk it over at yer council meetin'. I'll be passin' through here again in a day 'r two on the train, an' I'll look ya up. I'll be talkin' this over with my brothers too. Nice ta meet ya, Mayor Coates."

Charlie and his brothers left the saloon and jumped back into the Model T. As they rumbled out of town with the dogs barking and the fenders rattling, Charlie took a serious look around the town. They were all quiet, and no one brought up the conversation between the mayor and Charlie, or what had taken place in the saloon. Usually after a fight, they were full of chatter, telling each other how tough they were.

As they headed out of town, Charlie looked around thinking about what taking the job as the village marshal would be like and whether or not Lucy would want to move away from Mexico. The sun hung low in the sky, throwing off reflections of red and yellow. Hillview did not look any different from the other little towns he had been in, but from what had happened in the saloon that afternoon, and from what Mayor Coates had said, he knew that being the village marshal would not be an easy job.

CHAPTER 12

Fateful Decision

At the edge of town, Jim pulled the car over and let the dogs out of their pen. The dogs thought it was time to go hunting, so they bounded out of the pen and ran off into the trees at the side of the road. Jim had only traded one of the dogs that afternoon. The other two had been trained to come to him at the sound of the whistle he carried in his pocket. After a long shrill sound from the whistle, all three ran back to Jim. Right then he knew he had traded for a good dog. The new one followed the other two and was learning fast. They ran around him in circles, yelping and jumping. Dick and Ernest sat down on the running board of the car while Charlie and Jim worked to get the dogs back into the pen. Charlie knew his brothers were waiting for him to bring up the matter of the mayor's conversation.

"I'm sure ya heard what the mayor said 'bout bein' the village marshal back there. Seems like Hillview has a problem with that bunch o' ruffians, an' a few more just like 'em who 're givin' everybody a lot a trouble. You saw what happened today. Nobody'd want ta stop while passin' through 'r live in Hillview very long with those troublemakers. I been thinkin' 'bout what the mayor said. I'm goin' back there in a few days, an' I'll see what 'im an' the village council think 'bout me bein' the village marshal an' hear what else they have ta say. I'd only be the marshal if you three want ta be my deputies. He told me what the pay was, an' I'd pay you two dollars a day fer the days you work, an' give ya time off fer huntin' an' trappin'. Jus' as long as I have a couple of ya 'round all the time."

No one said anything for a few minutes, and the silence hung thick in the air. The day started out just to go look at hunting dogs but had taken a turn that no one could have expected. Dick was the first one to break the silence and said, "I'm game if ya are, Charlie. What 'bout ya two? Might be fun ta go over there an' clean up that town." Dick was always ready for a little excitement and adventure.

Jim and Ernest were a little hesitant in their responses and glanced at Charlie with worrisome looks.

Finally, Ernest said, "I got two questions. Do I have ta carry a gun, an' when do they want us ta start?"

Charlie did not respond but just waited to see what Jim was going to say.

Jim felt everyone's eyes on him and finally said, "Well if ya all want ta try ta clean up Hillview, I'm not goin' ta be left behind."

Charlie looked at his three brothers and mulled over what each of them had said. He looked at Ernest and said, "I don't carry a gun on the railroad, an' I don't think we need ta carry guns in Hillview. Not sure when they'd want me ta start. We didn't git that fer, but I think it'd have ta be a couple o' months. I'd need ta quit my railroad job, an' we'd have ta find us a place ta live in Hillview. That'll give us enough time ta git that done an' take care of our affairs in Mexico. Dick, you'd have ta quit yer job at the brickyard. I'll be goin' through Hillview in a couple a days. I'll stop an' talk ta Mayor Coates an' see what he thinks after he's had some time ta think 'bout his offer. He said he had ta talk ta the village council. Hell, he might be havin' second thoughts by now. I think it's time we be gittin' back to Mexico. We're goin' ta miss supper, but maybe there'll be somethin' kept warm we can eat. Lucy'll be mad that we didn't git back in time if she cooked a big supper."

CHAPTER 13

The Official Offer

A few days later, the train Charlie was working on made one of its regular stops at the Hillview station. Charlie had been thinking a lot about his talk with Mayor Coates and had mentioned it to Lucy. She had a dozen questions. and he did not have very good answers. He had decided he would get the matter of being village marshal settled one way or the other as soon possible, so he got off when the train made its stop in Hillview. He knew there was another train later on in the evening going back to Mexico that he could hop back on to get home. It did not take Charlie long to find the mayor. When he hopped off the train and walked into the station, he saw the mayor at the telegraph office, which was inside the station door.

When Mayor Coates saw Charlie, his face broke into a grin. "I wondered if you would come back. I didn't know if you were really serious, or if you would have second thoughts about my offer." The mayor told him that the village council was going to rely on his opinion of Charlie. He would like to offer Charlie the job as their village marshal. Charlie told the mayor he would accept the job, and that his brothers would be his deputies. They would be willing to start in a couple of months. The mayor told Charlie that the council members did want to meet him before the appointment became final though. They wanted to know what his ideas were about how he was going to clean up the violence in their town.

Charlie did not have a problem meeting with the village council. The mayor told Charlie to come back on the following Tuesday. Charlie spent the rest of the day ambling around Hillview, talking to a few of the townspeople and trying to get a feel for what was going on while he waited for the train back to Mexico. Once he got back home, he had a serious talk with Lucy and his parents about his plans.

A special council meeting was held the next week for Charlie to meet with them. He took the train back to Hillview early that morning. As Charlie walked into an upstairs room at the Phoenix Hotel where the meeting was being held, he saw the four council members and the mayor waiting for him. He shook hands with each council member, introduced himself, and abruptly began to address the group. He had mulled this over and thought he needed to tell them straightforwardly what his thoughts were. It seemed that the town needed him a whole lot more than he needed the job. He already had a good job. He had not been looking for another one when he met Mayor Coates in the saloon.

"The last time I came over here, I talked ta some o' the townsfolk before I left, an' I got a pretty good idea o' what the problem is. Ya got a bunch o' hoodlums who think they kin harass people an' run this town. I don't know how this happened, but if ya want me ta take care o' this problem, you'll have me let me do it my way. These thugs have run off all yer law people, an' they're runnin' loose. That won't happen with me. I won't be handlin' 'em with kid gloves, so ya have ta decide how bad ya want yer town cleaned up. Ya know who these thugs are, so if I do my job right, I might be steppin' on some toes that ya don't want stepped on. Ya had better decide before ya hire me who's goin' ta run this town—me an' you 'r them. If ya let me do the job right, I'll clean up the town, but I cain't do it halfway. If I start steppin' on toes then yer goin' ta start wonderin' if ya should a hired me in the first place. You'd better decide what ya want before ya hire me. I got a good job now with the railroad. I don't want ta quit my job an' move my family here if you're not goin' ta let me do the job the right way."

Charlie looked at each one of them in the eye and said, "Have I made myself clear?"

The council members appeared to be stunned. After a few moments of total silence, he stared at the council members and said, "Do any of ya have any questions?"

The council members and the mayor looked at each other, and not one of them said a word. They had not expected a stranger to walk in and be so blunt. Not getting a response, Charlie turned to leave and said, "I'll be over in the saloon fer a little while havin' a drink while ya make up yer minds. If you still want ta hire me as yer marshal, you know where ta find me. We can talk about a startin' time then. If not, it was nice meetin' y'all. I'll be catchin' the one-o'clock train outta here." Charlie turned, walked out of the room, and headed to the saloon. It was too early for a drink, but he would hang around for a little while.

Charlie was known by his family and friends to be a man of few words. His speech to the council members was probably more than what he had said at any one time in his life, especially to a bunch of strangers. About thirty minutes later, the heavy wooden door of the saloon swung open, and Mayor Coates walked in. As soon as he spotted Charlie, he walked up to the bar, and a big grin spread over his face. "Congratulations, Marshal Witwer."

Hillview, 1913

CHAPTER 14

Hillview

Hillview, located in Greene County, was established in 1892 and was originally named Pegram. In 1898, it was incorporated with the name of Happyville, and then again in 1903 was reincorporated and the name was changed to Hillview. Charles Wells, one of the local businesspersons, picked the name of Hillview. By 1913, Hillview had a population of over 630 people. It was a growing community, just east of what some residents called the "badlands." The badlands was property in the river bottom that was notorious for flooding. When it was not flooded, it was prime farming ground.

Hillview was a typical small Midwestern town. Early in 1900, some of the more well to do residents in the area had automobiles, but most people traveled by horseback, horse and buggy, a horse-drawn wagon, or by passenger train. Many local people used the passenger train to travel to other nearby towns. The train went through Hillview four times a day, so it was an easy way to travel. The train also brought many visitors and businesspersons to Hillview.

Four miles west of Hillview was a ferry that took people, wagons, and cars across the river to Pearl, Illinois. The road to the ferry quite often was not passable in an automobile or a wagon. When this occurred, if you needed to go to Pearl, you would have to travel down the road to the next ferry. Ten miles to the east of Hillview was the small town of White Hall, which was accessible on a poor gravel road. The county seat of Greene County was located in Carrollton, which was about ten miles south of White Hall. Most of the time, the gravel road to Carrollton was in good shape. The bluff road south of Hillview was quite often flooded, making travel in that direction impossible. Needless to say, many times the river had its grip on Hillview, making life difficult.

In the early 1900s, Hillview was a prosperous little village with numerous businesses. Hurricane Creek ran between Railroad Street and the railroad track. Most of the businesses were situated along Railroad Street—Adam's Hardware, Well's Grocery Store, Mrs. Greene's Restaurant, Corban Blacksmith Shop, Humboldt Patterson's Grocery, the Phoenix Hotel, Hillview State Bank, Angel's Grocery, the Apollo Theater, Ballard's Barbershop, Sam Layel's Pool Hall, Lacrosse Lumber Company, Binder's Garage, Garvin's Grocery and Drug Store, Humble Blacksmith Shop, H. C. Drug Store, Ballard's Filling Station, and Ray Crosby Poultry. Railroad Street was not only a place to do your shopping, but it was a place for the locals to socialize.

In addition to these businesses, there were at least three saloons frequented by the men of the village and surrounding area. Of course, women did not go to the saloons. It was thought that women and alcohol were a bad combination and would create problems for the saloon owners. An occasional argument could be heard in one of the saloons, and every once in a while a fight did break out, but for the most part, they were gathering places for the locals to talk about what was going on around town and to play cards while having a drink. If there was any serious trouble, it was usually caused by some of the young fellows who were mostly unemployed and spent their time drinking and looking for a fight to pick. It was well known that one or two of them would hop the train daily to travel over the state line to Missouri to buy alcohol and bring it back to the others. They then would roam around the village drinking and terrorizing the residents and people at the train station.

Sometimes there was a band of hoodlums from one of the small surrounding towns that came to Hillview and harassed the residents. To make matters worse, they sometimes squabbled with the local hoodlums. These bands of hoodlums were often referred to as "river rats." It was common knowledge that Hillview, and the surrounding small towns of Patterson and Walkerville, had a very high rate of unsolved crimes and so-called "accidental deaths."

In May of 1902, a body was found on the railroad tracks and was in such a poor condition that it could not be identified. In April of 1903, a drowning in a well occurred, and in August of 1903, another body was found on the railroad tracks. The local law officer had no conclusive evidence of how any of these deaths occurred. In 1904, one death was determined to be a suicide by drowning in well, but many of the local residents believed it was foul play rather than a suicide. In November of 1908, another body was found on the railroad tracks, and in December of 1910, there was a murder by gunshot. In May of 1912, the headlines read, "Death by Drowning." Even though Hillview was a prosperous, growing village, its reputation for violence and mayhem was well known.

Hillview was known for having the largest privately owned apple orchard in the United States, known as the McClay Apple Orchard. When it was time to pick the fruit in the fall, Mr. McClay hired as many as one hundred to four hundred seasonal migrant workers, depending on the size of the harvest for that year. These migrant workers were housed in a large boarding house, which sat on a hill on the north side of Hillview. It had a dining room that could hold up to two hundred workers at one time.

Having that many migrant workers descend on the village created its own set of problems when it came to keeping the peace. The local ruffians only made the situation worse. They would buy alcohol in Missouri and then sell it to the migrant workers at a higher price. The McClay family strenuously objected to this, but no one seemed to be able to do much about it.

CHAPTER 15

Moving to Hillview

As the Model T chugged along toward Hillview, Charlie pondered the responsibility he had for moving almost his whole family, first his brothers and then his wife. He wondered if it would be long before his mom and dad would want to move to Hillview and maybe even move in with them. If this occurred, he did not know if their little brother, Harry, would want to move with them. Jacob and Nancy liked being close to their boys. Being the oldest son had always put him in a position where his brothers, and even Jacob and Nancy, looked to him to make decisions. He never shirked from this responsibility.

Once they left Mexico that November morning, Charlie had not paid much attention to the conversation the other three were having. After being on the road for a few hours, Jim found a place for them to pull over so they could eat the dinner Lucy and Liz had packed. It was a little early to eat but the sun was shining brightly, and they were glad to get out and stretch their legs. Riding in that Model T had given them all a chill. They were glad for the warmth of the sun on their backs as they sat with a piece of chicken in one hand and a biscuit in the other looking at the bare, fertile fields around them. The corn had been harvested, so the fields were full of corn stubble. They did not spend much time eating their dinner, as they were anxious to get to Hillview.

The biggest part of the trip was over, but they figured they still had about an hour to drive to get to the ferry at Pearl to cross the river, so they piled back into the car, pulling their caps down over their ears. It was not too long before Dick's hollering jerked Charlie out of his thoughts and back to the road. Charlie squinted his eyes and looked through the dirty windshield to see what Dick was hollering about. As his eyes spanned the horizon, he could see Hillview across the river and down the road in front of them. The houses were not much more than tiny dots, but he knew Hillview was not too far away. Dick continued hollering at Charlie and poking him on the shoulder, even though no one seemed to be paying attention to him. He was excited to see Hillview and wanted to know where the house was that they were going to be living in. Charlie told Dick to settle down, and he would give Jim directions when they got closer.

Once Charlie had accepted the position of village marshal, one of the first things he did was make a couple of trips to Hillview to rent a house for all of them to move into. Houses to rent were not plentiful, especially one big enough for the four brothers and Lucy. Charlie did not have many from which to choose. He finally found one big enough to keep them all together, even if it was in need of some repairs.

As the car rumbled along and approached the outskirts of town, Charlie told Jim to turn east on Railroad Street, turn right on Main Street, go over the railroad track, pass the railroad station, and the house would be on the corner of Main and Maple. That was far too much information for Jim to remember, so after a couple of wrong turns they finally got on the right street. Jim pulled up in front of the house, rolled into the driveway, and stopped the car with a jerk. The driveway looked like it might have had some gravel on it at one time, but there was little to be seen that day. As they pulled into driveway, they saw the one-story house Charlie had directed them to.

Jim took one look at it and groaned, "I hope ya rented this thing cheap. The gutters fallin' off an' the paint's peelin'. The screen door looks like its hangin' off its hinges. I bet the grass ain't been mowed since the middle o' summer. That grass is so high the dogs might git lost in it. I hope it looks better inside than on the outside."

Ernest and Dick just sat staring at their new home. They both knew it was best not to say a word; Jim had already said all that needed to be said.

"I know it ain't much ta look at, but it has a few things in its favor. As ya can see, we're sittin' up here on a hill an' can see the whole downtown part of Hillview, includin' the jailhouse. I was told that Hillview gits some serious floodin' from Hurricane Creek an' the river, an' we're way above both of 'em. So, jus' quit yer complainin' an' git outta the car."

Jim shut the engine off, and the dogs immediately started barking. They were ready to get out of their pen. Jim put a chain on each one of them before he let them run out. He grabbed the sack of bones he had brought with him and headed around the house to the backyard with the barking dogs. They jerked him along and did not seem the least bit concerned that the grass and weeds were rubbing their bellies. They were just happy to be out of that pen. They were making so much noise that if the neighbors heard the ruckus and looked out, it was quite a comical scene.

In the backyard, Jim found an old, sagging clothesline held up by two rickety metal posts leaning in opposite directions. He hoped those posts would stay in the ground with the dogs hooked to them until he had time to fix them. After he had the dogs securely hooked to the clothesline pole, he opened the bag and threw the bones to them. Each dog immediately quit barking, pounced on a bone, and started gnawing on it. That would keep them quiet for a little while. As Jim looked around the yard and at the back of the house, he could see there was going to be a lot of fixing up to do. The grass was so high in the yard you could hardly see the dogs as they lay chewing on the bones. Jim headed back around to the front of the house muttering that he needed to get a pen built for his dogs. Building that pen would be a priority for Jim, no matter what Charlie wanted him to do.

By the time Jim got back to the front of the house, Charlie, Ernest, and Dick had gotten out of the car and were standing in the yard stretching their legs, looking around at the neighborhood. It looked a lot like their street back in Mexico—brown grass, rutted yards, houses with the paint peeling, rickety porches, crooked sidewalks, and a dog meandering down the middle of the street. Their house in Mexico was not fancy, but it did look better than the one Charlie had rented. It was the worst one in the neighborhood!

Ernest and Dick looked up at the roof and then looked at each other. Neither one had to say a word. They were each wondering what would happen when the first rain came along. Would they wake up some night with drips coming from the ceiling and landing on their heads? They were hoping the inside looked a whole lot better than the outside.

As they stood there, they heard the train whistle in the distance. The whistle got louder and louder as it approached the railroad station, and it hardly slowed down as it went through Hillview. The rumbling of the wheels made so much noise the windows in the house seemed to rattle. Jim looked at Charlie and said, "That damn train whistle is makin' my dogs howl. It must hurt their ears, 'cause it sure as hell hurts mine. I sure hope I don't have ta hear that when I'm sleepin'."

Charlie just looked at Jim and replied, "You'll git used to it. Must a been a freight train 'cause it didn't stop.

Didn't even slow down much. I know this ain't the fanciest house, but I think it'll do. We kin clean up the yard an' fix a few things. It won't be the first time we've had ta fix somethin' up."

Charlie walked up the cracked front sidewalk and up the front steps that let out a groan with every step he took. He looked for the key on the ledge above the door where the landlord said he would put it. Finding it, he put it into the keyhole and swung the door open. "Well, fellas, come on in an' take a look at yer new home."

Jim, Ernest, and Dick followed Charlie into the house with a great deal of skepticism showing on their faces. They had never lived in a fancy house, but this house sure did look rough. As each of them meandered through, poking their heads into each of the rooms, their impressions of the house did not get any better. There was a front room, a kitchen, three rooms that could be used for bedrooms, and a closed-in back porch. They knew that the back porch was where the washtub would be and probably where they would be taking their Saturday night baths. There was another room stuck on the side of the house that looked like it had been added on sometime after the house was built. Looking out the window that was in the back door, they could see the outhouse about twenty feet away and the remains of a path that had become overgrown with grass and weeds. The house had no indoor plumbing, but they were used to that. They would definitely need to get all of those weeds cut down in the backyard so they could get to the outhouse. Of course, during the night they usually did not make trips to the outhouse but made use of a "slop jar" they kept in their bedrooms. The only bad thing about that slop jar was that no one wanted to be the one to empty it.

As they looked around, they saw that the wallpaper was peeling in the corners and hanging down in some of the rooms. It looked like somebody had put some thumbtacks in a few places. One bedroom had crayon marks on the wall, evidently made by a child that had lived there at one time. The wooden floors had large cracks in them and squeaked noisily with every few steps. If anyone came in late, those creaking floors would wake everyone. The kitchen had a large wood-burning cooking stove and an icebox with one broken leg. Someone had put a brick under the corner of it to hold it up. The kitchen was sparsely furnished with a large table. Lots of scratches and dents on the top of the table showed that other occupants had used it for many meals. When you're hungry and sitting down to a meal, though, it did not matter how many scratches there were on the tabletop. Charlie figured Lucy would throw a cloth over it to hide the top anyway. Chairs were scattered around the room, some with broken spindles in the back, but at least there were eight chairs.

Against one wall in the living room sat a threadbare, gray couch with a couple of overstuffed chairs against the other wall. A large potbellied stove for burning wood or coal sat opposite of the couch. This stove and the cook stove in the kitchen would provide heat for the house.

Each of the three bedrooms had a double bed with feather mattresses on top of the metal springs and pillows piled on top. There was a nightstand by each bed with a kerosene lamp on top of it. They knew that after a cold night, when the fire burned low in the potbellied stove, there would be frost on the inside of the single-paned windows, particularly in these bedrooms. On these nights, each of the men would have to wear their long underwear and socks to stay warm. Women in the household would have to wear their warmest flannel nightgown and socks. There would be no leisurely getting out of bed in the morning and sitting on the edge to stretch. They would stay warm during the night as the feather mattresses folded up around them with plenty of blankets piled on top, but once the blankets were thrown back and their feet hit the icy floor, they would feel the cold envelop them. No one would tarry in getting dressed and would hope that someone else had started a fire in the potbellied stove.

The room that had been added onto the side of the house had been used as a bedroom at one time. In it were two cots, side by side. Like the other bedrooms, feather mattresses and pillows were piled on top of the metal springs, and a nightstand with a kerosene lamp stood between the two cots. There was a small window on each side of the room. As each brother went into the back bedroom, he was hoping he was not the one that would be sleeping there. This small room would be a lot colder in the winter months because it was the farthest away from the potbellied stove and hotter in the summer with only two little windows. With as many beds as there were in the house, it must have been a large family that had once lived there. They knew Charlie was going to take one of the bedrooms in the main part of the house, so who were going to be the lucky ones to get the other bedrooms? It did not take Dick long to pick out the bedroom he wanted—just in case, he talked Liz into coming to Hillview! Ernest and Jim were trying to figure out how they could avoid being the one in the little side room, but they sure did not want to share a room.

There were no curtains on any of the windows, but Charlie was not concerned about curtains. He knew Lucy would take care of that as soon as he brought her to Hillview. She might even get busy on those curtains if she finds out that they do not have any.

Ernest walked back through the closed-in porch and out into the backyard through the tall grass looking for the well. As he stumbled across the well platform and nearly fell down, he hollered, "I found the damn well but there ain't no pump handle."

Jim followed Ernest outside and laughed as he said, "You don't take that many baths anyway." Ernest just glared back at Jim and mumbled something under his breath.

Charlie, who had been walking around the side of the house hollered at them, "Quit worryin'. I see the pump handle leanin' here against the house an' a pipe fer the well. We'll git it workin' 'fore we go ta bed tonight."

Ernest looked around for a woodpile thinking that before nightfall they would need to be firing up the potbellied stove. It was getting colder, and the wind had picked up. It was turning into a raw, cold wind, and you could hear it whistling through the branches that had lost their leaves. He spotted a small pile of wood next to the house. "There's a small pile o' wood we can use tonight, but we're goin' ta have ta cut some more 'fore long. I'm sure we packed the saw an' ax."

As the brothers went back into the house through the back room, Jim said, "I don't think Lucy's goin' ta like that flowered wallpaper in the front room. You'd better git yer paint brush ready, Charlie."

Charlie just glared at him and said, "Don't ya worry none 'bout what Lucy likes an' don't like. When she gits over here, she'll make this place look good. We'll git some things fixed up 'fore she gits here. I don't want her ta be too disappointed with this house."

Hillview Jail, 1914

CHAPTER 16

The Hillview Jail

There were a couple of daylight hours left, so Jim's thoughts turned to his dogs. They were still tied to the clothesline pole in the backyard. He needed to buy some lumber and materials to get a pen built for them. As he turned to Charlie, he said, "Did ya tell me there was a lumberyard in this town?"

"Yeah, there's LaCrosse Lumber Company here an' maybe 'nother one too. I need ta go find the mayor an' walk 'round town a little. Maybe meet some more o' the business owners. Why don't ya drive me downtown, an' I'll find the mayor while ya find the lumber company. Ya just come on back ta the house when ya buy yer lumber, and I'll walk on back ta the house. It ain't that fer."

Jim dropped Charlie off in front of Humboldt Patterson's Store and then drove the Model T around the corner to the lumberyard. Charlie had been in Patterson's on one of his previous trips to Hillview but decided to take a few minutes to look around and see what all was on the shelves and sitting on the floor. There was a large plate-glass window by the front door that displayed several bolts of fabric and a pair of boots. The shelves inside were crammed full of household and personal care items. Charlie concluded that if you did not find what you wanted in this store, you probably did not need it. Charlie knew that the store would be a gathering place for the townspeople as they came to do their shopping. Mr. Patterson knew how to take care of his customers. He had put a couple of benches outside for the fellas to sit on while the women did their shopping.

Charlie also knew that this was one of the places to hear the local gossip. If anything went on in the community, you could probably find out about it in Humboldt Patterson's Store. He could hear the buzz of conversation as he strolled through the aisles and through the plate-glass window could see the men nodding their heads as they listened to one another. Charlie recognized Mr. Patterson and saw him standing behind the counter. He did not have a customer to take care of at that moment, so Charlie took the opportunity to introduce himself.

"I'm Charlie Witwer an' I'm goin' ta be yer new marshal. Just got ta town today, an' thought I would meet some o' the townsfolk."

"Nice to meet you. I've heard some good things about you from the mayor. We sure need a good marshal. Any help I can give you, you just let me know, and if you need anything in the store, we're open six days a week. As you can see, we have just about anything you might need."

"Thanks. Ya sure do have a lot of things on yer shelves. I am sure me an' my brothers will be seein' ya a lot. Right now, though, the first help you kin give me is ta tell me where I kin find Mayor Coates."

"Go two doors down on your right just past Greene's Restaurant. I think I saw him going into the Phoenix Hotel a few minutes ago."

"Nice ta have met ya. By the way, I need ta set up a post office box too. I heard you're the postmaster here in Hillview.

"Yeah, I sure am. I can take care of that right now if you want to. We just need to fill out this form with your address here in Hillview and then get your signature on the form."

Charlie looked at the form, scratched his head, and said, "There ain't a number on the house."

"Don't worry about that. You can just have people send mail to you care of 'General Delivery,' and you can pick it up right here."

That sounded good to Charlie, so he took care of that business, tipped his hat to Mr. Patterson, and walked out.

As Charlie approached the Phoenix Hotel, he saw a new two-story frame structure with a small but ornate lobby. A sofa and two chairs were in the lobby area for guests to use. He had not been in many hotels but would soon learn that the Phoenix Hotel had twelve rooms for guests with a common toilet on each floor. Each room was cheery and bright with quilts on the bed, and on the nightstand in each room stood a porcelain water pitcher and bowl. There was a bathhouse in the rear of the hotel, which had a separate area for men and women. Not many people had a bathroom in their house, so that bathhouse was quite a topic of conversation. Hillview residents were proud of the Phoenix Hotel and boasted about it. Most of the people who stayed at the Phoenix Hotel were travelers who were traveling on the train. Popular travel destinations were Kansas City and Chicago, and many of the travelers stayed overnight in the small towns at which the train stopped. Four passenger trains a day stopped in Hillview, so the hotel had a booming business.

As Charlie entered the hotel, Mayor Coates was standing in front of the registration desk talking to the desk clerk. It did not take Charlie long to find out that Mayor Coats spent quite a bit of time in the lobby of the Phoenix Hotel. The mayor turned as he heard the door open. When he saw Charlie, he walked over and said, "Are you ready to go to work? I see you've got your cane with you."

"Yeah, I'm ready, an' yeah, I got my cane with me. I don't go very many places without my cane. We just got in here this afternoon. Ya might give me a day 'r two ta git some things taken care o' at the house, an' then I'll be ready. My brothers came with me. They're goin' ta be my deputies, so they'll be ready too. I suppose ya need ta swear me an' my deputies in before we start workin'."

"Not really. The council already authorized you to be appointed as the village marshal, so I just need to show you around a bit. As I told you, you can name whomever you want to as your deputies. I'm glad your brothers came with you. Why don't you come over to the jail right now, and I'll give you the key. That's where your office will be. You can pick up your badges and some handcuffs when you start in a couple of days."

"That sounds good. I was hopin' ta see the jail. I plan on usin' it when necessary."

Charlie and the mayor walked a short distance to the jail. As Charlie entered the two-story structure, to his left he saw two cells. Each one had two cots with thin straw mattresses on top. A metal slop jar was sitting in the corner of each cell. Straight across from the front door was what he assumed to be an entrance from the back. As he opened the back door, an unbearable stench came from the two-holed outhouse that sat a few feet behind the jail. The door was ajar, and you could see an old catalog on the bench seat with half of the pages torn out. Someone had evidently been using the old outhouse quite a bit! An old well was at the corner of the jail but the rusty pump had no handle.

A potbellied coal stove sat in one corner not too far from a scarred wooden desk. A rusty register was in the ceiling, which would let a small amount of the warm air drift up to the second floor. It would be cold up there on a winter day. The only light source, other than the windows, came from a single light bulb hanging down on an electrical cord that hung from the ceiling. There were three windows, which had bars on them, across one side of the building opposite of the cells. Charlie could see that one of the windows could be opened for air. He knew that since they were in a river bottom, the mosquitoes were probably as big as horseflies. It was obvious to Charlie that the jail had not been used for some time. Everything was dusty, and cobwebs hung from the ceiling. He would have to do some cleaning before he could use it. He would put those brothers of his to work very quickly!

Charlie looked around for a few minutes and said, "What's upstairs?"

"Well, there's some space up there for an office, and the circuit judge might use it as his courtroom. But, you can see from the dust and cobwebs, there's not been anybody in here for a while. To get upstairs, you have to take the stairs outside. Would you like to go up there?"

"No, I don't need ta go right now. My deputies an' I will be tryin' ta clean this place up a bit. Are there any mops 'r brooms around?"

"I don't know if there are any around here right now, but I'll make sure to get some in here tomorrow. Anything else you need, you just let me know."

"If I put somebody in one of those cells, how do I feed 'em?"

"Just go down to Mrs. Greene's Restaurant and tell her what you need whenever you have anybody in here. She knows we'll settle up with her at the end of the week."

"That sounds okay, but does that come outta my pay? If these cells git full, I might not be able ta feed myself after feedin' 'em."

The mayor laughed as he handed Charlie a key and replied, "I can understand your concern. Feeding anybody that you put in those cells will not come out of your pay."

"Thanks fer the key. I'll be here in a few days. I might even be here day after tomorrow. Just depends on what we git done on the house tomorrow. There'll be four of us workin', so we can git things done pretty quick."

They both walked out of the jail, and Charlie locked the door with his newly acquired key. Mayor Coates headed across the street, and Charlie strolled back toward the hotel. It was getting late in the day, but he spent a little more time looking around and introducing himself to a couple of the business owners. Everyone he spoke to seemed friendly and enthusiastic about his appointment as the village marshal, but he occasionally felt that the enthusiasm was not as sincere as it sounded. That left him a little perplexed and very curious about what this new job was going to be like.

CHAPTER 17

The Ringleaders

As Charlie stood on the wooden walk in front of Greene's Restaurant, he could see that the golden sun hung low in the sky, so it would be dark before long. The temperature was dropping, and he had not dressed warm enough to be out much longer. Their house was not far from the downtown area, though, so he decided to walk to the railroad station before he headed home and say hello to the ticket agent. As he got closer to the station, he saw a group of loud, boisterous young men sitting on the platform and milling around. They were passing a bottle around, which Charlie guessed, from the way they were acting and the noise they were making, was a bottle of whiskey. Without being too conspicuous, Charlie slowed his pace so he could watch what was going on. About that time, a tall, blond-headed fellow shoved one of the others.

As the blond-haired person staggered around, he fell against a woman who was trying to enter the station house. The group just laughed and hollered something to the woman that Charlie could not hear. Charlie figured these were some of the ruffians he had been hearing about. He looked back over his shoulder and saw Mr. Patterson locking up his store for the night, so he turned and walked back to the store.

"Mr. Patterson, who're those fellas over there at the railroad station with the bottle?"

Mr. Patterson could hear some hollering and looked over in the direction of the railroad station. He squinted his eyes and said, "It looks like Bum Deeds, Isom Leonard, and their buddies. I can't see well enough to see who the others are, but I'm sure they're some of the ones that cause a lot of trouble around here."

Charlie took another good look in that direction and asked, "Does Deeds have a first name 'r is Bum his first name? 'Cause that's what he's actin' like!"

"No, he's got a first name but everybody just calls him Bum. He and Leonard are sort of the ringleaders of those gangs of ruffians that cause the trouble around here. There's a bunch of them, but you can almost bet that Deeds and Leonard will always be two of them."

"Thanks fer the information. I'm sure it'll come in handy."

Charlie turned up the collar on his coat and headed back up the street to the house. When he got there, Jim was still working on the dog pen although it was almost dark. Ernest and Dick had been working on the pump handle and had used the little bit of firewood to start a fire in the potbellied stove. He was glad to feel the warmth as he walked in the front door, as the wind was beginning to pick up. He had an idea it was going to be cold night and hoped they had enough firewood to get through the night.

Charlie walked on through the house and out the back door. Jim looked up and said, "I got acquainted with the neighbor that lives in that house over there. I think you'll like 'im, Charlie. He tol' me he has several ridin' horses an' a team he uses fer plowin' 'r pullin' his wagon. He lent me a hammer an' saw since I didn't have one handy. Ours is still packed in the car. Gave me a box a nails too 'cause I forgot ta buy 'em. I told 'im the first chance I had ta go huntin' with the dogs, he could go along."

"I look forward to meetin' 'im. Let's go git Ernest an' Dick. Its dark and gittin' colder by the minute. That chicken an' biscuits Lucy sent with us fer dinner was good but I'm hungry. Been a long time since we ate. We ain't got no groceries yet so I think we'd better head back ta Mrs. Greene's Restaurant an' git somethin' ta eat. They might be closin' 'fore long, so let's git a move on it."

"Should we walk 'r drive?"

"It's cold but it ain't that fer. Let's just walk so hurry it up."

CHAPTER 18

Mrs. Greene's Restaurant

By the time the four brothers left for the restaurant, there were no clouds in the sky, and the full moon was providing light as they made their way to Mrs. Greene's. They hurried along so they could get there before closing time. By this time everyone's stomachs were growling, and doing without supper was not something any of them wanted to do.

Jim said, "This kind o' weather should cause the fur ta prime early, so trappin' should be good this year. We'll have ta git back ta Mexico 'fore trappin' season starts an' bring back the traps."

Dick said, "That's a good idea. Maybe we can go over on the train. Might be quicker, an' we can carry the traps back on the train. I can see Liz when we go. Got ta see if that Cookie fella has been hangin' 'round."

Jim shook his head and grinned at Charlie. "You just want ta git over there 'fore that Cookie guy gits ahead o' ya with Liz. With you bein' gone, she jus' might fall fer 'im"

"I'm not worried 'bout that. He ain't never goin' ta git ahead o' me. I just want ta see Liz"

As they walked, Charlie listened to their chatter and thought they would not have much time for hunting or trapping for a while. They had a lot of work to do around the house and cleaning up the jail. He was sure he was going to need them to help keep the streets of Hillview safe. He had told his brothers he would give them time off to go hunting and trapping, so he would have to figure out some sort of schedule. He was not sure yet just how things were going to work out, but he figured he needed at least one or two of them available most of the time. He thought that if there was going to be trouble in town, it would be in the late afternoon or the evenings. They most always went hunting in the morning so that would help.

If what he had heard about one or two of the troublemakers heading to Missouri to buy liquor for the others was true, then they probably hung around all afternoon drinking and were ready to stir up trouble later in the day. Charlie did not know of any way to stop them from coming back with their "fightin' whiskey," but he sure was going to have to figure out a way to keep them from roaming the streets of Hillview causing trouble.

As they walked down the walkway to Mrs. Greene's, they could see though the windows that there was not much of a crowd. It was getting late, and most of her customers had already had their supper and left. As they entered the door, they saw plenty of open tables and chairs. Jim headed to a table on the side of the room where they could look out a window, and the other three followed. They all took off their hats and coats and hung them on the wooden coat rack that was standing in the corner of the room. The few people sitting at other tables turned and nodded as they passed by.

Mrs. Greene's Restaurant had a counter with five stools and six tables with chairs. On the wall in front of the counter was a chalkboard where the menu for the day was written, along with what was on special for that day. They could see that a couple of items had been scratched off, but, at this time of night, they were not going to be picky about what they ate. The floor was well-worn green and white linoleum, which did not blend well with the green walls. Green and white checkered curtains covered only the bottom half of the windows that faced the street, so you could still see the people walking by. Once a person was in Mrs. Greene's Restaurant, it was hard to forget it—or to forget the name of it! Most everything was green!

The glass-covered shelf behind the counter still had a couple of pieces of pie on it. In the back corner was a large coal-and-wood-burning stove with a large black pot sitting on the top. The special for the day was ham and beans. The pot was still on the stove, so there must be some ham and beans left. Mrs. Greene was at the restaurant very early every morning before it opened to get all of the cooking and pie baking started. If Mrs. Greene was ill and unable to do the cooking, the "open" sign was not put in the window that day. That made for some very unhappy people, especially some of the single fellows in town who relied on getting a good meal at least once a day.

A couple of the women in town came in every morning when the restaurant opened and worked until the middle of the afternoon. Some days, Mrs. Greene would take some time off in the middle of the morning or the middle of the afternoon. Mrs. Greene hired high school girls to come in and help during the supper hour. Mrs. Greene's was definitely the place to go for some good home cooking and catching up on the latest gossip. It was a tossup as to where the most gossiping occurred, Mrs. Greene's Restaurant or Patterson's General Store.

As the four brothers sat down at the table, a robust woman with a big smile walked over. "Well, these must be your brothers you were tellin' me about when you stopped in this afternoon. We're glad to have you in town. We need somebody around here that will take care of these ruffians when they start causin' trouble. You got your work cut out for you."

Charlie replied, "These are my brothers, Jim, Ernest, an' Dick. They're goin' ta be my deputies, so I think we'll be able ta handle things."

"Well, I am glad you came in. The menu is on the chalkboard over there, so look it over and tell me what you want. Got a little bit of the special that's left, and I got some meatloaf that's mighty good. My own special recipe. I got just about enough left to feed you fellas. Just to welcome you to town, you won't have to pay for your supper tonight." With a chuckle, she said, "But don't be expectin' that the next time you come in!"

It did not take long for them to decide that the meatloaf sounded mighty good, and Mrs. Greene had their plates to them in just a few minutes. As they sat eating their meal, Charlie looked out between the green and white checkered curtains that had been pushed back on the curtain rod. He could see a couple of young men milling around on the sidewalk in front of the restaurant.

"We need ta watch our step goin' home after we eat. Not sure if those fellas out there 're lookin' fer trouble."

The three brothers peered out the window but could not see anyone in the shadows.

Dick replied, "Well, if they cause any trouble I hope they're the same ones we met in the bar the first time we came over here. I still ain't got that hole fixed in my pants that got ripped that day. Ya got yer cane with ya, Charlie?"

"Yeah, I got my cane with me. We don't want any trouble tonight, but we'll keep an eye out."

As they were taking their last bites, Mrs. Greene walked over to the table and looked directly at Dick. "Honey, could I interest you in a piece of chocolate pie? I made it myself this mornin'."

Dick was not easily flustered, but a color rose in his cheeks as he shoved his chair back while the other three tried to hide their smirks. "Uh, maybe some other time. That was a mighty good supper, an' I'm full as a tick."

They all pushed their chairs back from the table and thanked Mrs. Greene for her hospitality. They got their hats and coats and headed for the door. By this time, it was pitch dark and the shadows were deep. The streets were empty of people except for the young men who had moved to the other side of the street. They were sitting on a wooden bench with what looked like a bottle wrapped in a sack. All of the stores were closed for the night, and except for the moonlight, Hillview was dark.

As Charlie and his brothers started down the street, they heard one of the young men holler, “Heard we had a new marshal who brought some deputies with 'im. Are you those fellas? You made a big mistake comin’ here.”

Dick, who was always ready for a fight, said, “Are we goin’ ta let ’em git away with that?”

Charlie replied, “Just ignore ’em. This ain’t the time or the place ta start somethin’. They been drinkin’, an' we don’t need ta git in a fight the first night we’re here. I need ta talk ta the mayor tomorrow. I tol’ him we won’t be startin’ until day after tomorrow ’r the next day anyway.”

CHAPTER 19

The Handbills

The next morning Charlie met with the mayor and asked about whether or not there was an ordinance against public drunkenness in Hillview.

"Well, there's no such ordinance that I know of."

"If you want me ta git these thugs off the streets so they're not causin' trouble, then you got ta ask the village council if they'll pass an ordinance makin' it an offense ta be drunk in public, if ya don't already have one. Those troublemakers don't need ta be carryin' 'round a bottle, drinkin' on the streets an' just gittin' drunker."

"When the council meets tonight, I'll bring it up to them and see what they want to do about it. I'll come by your house after the meeting and let you know what they decide."

The village council did not make any changes in the city ordinances but advised the mayor that there was a disorderly conduct ordinance that should cover the act of being drunk. Mayor Coates walked to Charlie's house after the meeting. He told Charlie that Mr. Mundy, the president of the village council, said they discussed Charlie's request but came to the decision that they had enough ordinances on the books, and they did not need another one specifically addressing drunkenness. As Charlie mulled this over after the mayor left, he became somewhat perturbed at the attitude of the council. He wondered if some of those hoodlums causing trouble just might be related to some of them.

As was Charlie's habit when he had a problem, he put a cigar in his mouth and sat in a chair mulling the situation over. Before long, he came up with an idea and spent the next hour working on it.

Early the next morning, Charlie, cane in hand, and his three brothers headed to the jail. He decided this would be his first official day as the marshal, and he wanted to get started on the idea he had come up with after the mayor's visit the night before. He handed the key to the jail to Jim and told his three brothers to start cleaning up the jail while he went to find the mayor. Jim, Ernest and Dick did not think cleaning the jail was part of "deputy duties" but chose not to argue about it. They had watched Charlie the night before and knew that this was not the time to disagree with him.

As usual, Mayor Coates was not hard to find. Mayor Coates worked in the telegraph office, but when he was not at his job, he was usually at the Phoenix Hotel talking business with some of the merchants. As Charlie walked by the Phoenix Hotel, he looked through the window and spotted Mayor Coates talking to the desk clerk. Charlie walked in, handed him a piece of paper, and asked the mayor to read it. The mayor took the piece of paper and read what Charlie had written down.

ANYONE FOUND DRUNK ON A PUBLIC STREET IN HILLVIEW, ILLINOIS, WILL BE SUBJECT TO IMMEDIATE ARREST — CHARLES R. WITWER, VILLAGE MARSHAL

Charlie told Mayor Coates he wanted to get some handbills printed and posted around the village. Mayor Coates thought for a few minutes before replying, "I don't see any problem with this. You can take these to the newspaper office in White Hall and see if they can print them for you. Tell them I authorized for them to be printed."

Mayor Coates handed the piece of paper back to Charlie. Charlie thanked him and walked back to the jail. He was glad the mayor did not object to the handbills being printed because he was not going to back down. He was still perturbed about the incident the night before and decided they needed to get started on stopping these ruffians from harassing people.

Ernest was in front of the jail trying to sweep the dirt off the walk. Charlie handed Ernest the flier and said, "Go git the Model T an' take this ta the newspaper office in White Hall. See if they kin tell ya where ya kin git me twenty-five handbills printed up or if they kin do it. Tell 'em yer a deputy in Hillview, an' we need these as soon as we kin git 'em. Here's a couple o' dollars. I think this'll be plenty."

Ernest took off in a run. From the look on Charlie's face, he knew he had better not ask any questions and just do what he was told. He was tired of cleaning anyway. Jim and Dick could finish the job. Ernest did not have any trouble finding the newspaper office, which was on Main Street in White Hall. He parked the Model T and hurried through the front door, nearly knocking a little woman down that was coming out of the door. As he walked up to the counter, a man was coming through the doorway of a small room in the back. Ernest asked him if he was the editor of the newspaper.

"I sure am the editor. What can I do for you?"

"I'm a deputy in Hillview, an' we need ta git some handbills printed like this here. Kin ya do them fer us?"

The editor read the piece of paper Ernest handed to him. "I heard there was a new marshal and that he was bringin' some deputies with him. I know there's been trouble over there. Mayor Coates and I are good friends, so I'm glad to help out. If you come back in a couple of hours,

I'll see if I can get these printed for you. How many do you want?"

Ernest was relieved that things were going so smoothly. "I sure do 'preciate yer helpin' us out. I guess we need 'bout twenty-five. I'll be back in a couple o' hours."

Ernest roamed around White Hall, ducking into some of the businesses just to warm up. He was so glad Charlie asked him to make the trip to White Hall, and not Jim, that he forgot he would be missing a good meal at Mrs. Greene's Restaurant. He found the general store and bought some candy to chew on until he got back to Hillview

Ernest went back to the newspaper office in two hours, picked up the handbills and headed back to Hillview. Even though it was cold and the wind whistled through the Model T, it was better than cleaning that jail. He hoped Charlie, Jim, and Dick would have it done by the time he got back but he was not going to dawdle. He wanted to get there as quick as he could to see what Charlie was going to do with the handbills

Charlie, Dick, and Jim spent the rest of the day working at the jail, getting the cobwebs down and sweeping out the dirt and dust. Late in the afternoon, they heard the rumble of the Model T and looked out the window as Ernest parked it and jumped out waving the handbills.

"Damn, that Model T ain't very warm on a day like this. I nearly froze, but here, I got twenty-five of 'em printed, Charlie. Here's what's left over o' yer money. Now, what're we goin' ta do with 'em?"

"We're goin' ta post these everywhere we can. I want everybody ta know that we're not goin' ta tolerate anybody gittin' drunk an' causin' trouble. I call that disorderly conduct, an' there's a city ordinance sayin' disorderly conduct is against the law. I guess there ain't nobody ever enforced the law 'round here."

Marshal Charlie and his deputies spent the rest of the afternoon walking around posting handbills wherever they could, stirring up a lot of curiosity as they made their way around town. Some of the townsfolk wanted to know what it was all about and others just stepped aside and watched them being tacked up. Occasionally, they would find a business owner that would let them put one in the window or on the doorframe.

It was late when they got to Mrs. Greene's Restaurant, and it was beginning to spit snow. They were chilled to the bone and glad to get into the warmth. The restaurant was filled with tantalizing smells dancing through the air. After having nothing but candy at noon, Ernest was starving by the time they headed to Mrs. Greene's. They still did not have anything to eat at the house, but that was okay because nobody wanted to cook anyway. After eating, they walked back down to the jail where the Model T was sitting. Ice crystals had formed on the windshield. Jim turned the crank to get it started. They were all tired and glad for the ride home, even if it was cold. There was a dusting of snow, but it looked like that was all there would be, as they could see a few stars in the dark sky. They did not encounter anyone on the street, so they thought that maybe it would be a peaceful night.

The next morning, as Charlie and the three brothers walked downtown, they saw a handbill wadded up and thrown into the street. Charlie told them to spread out and see if all of the handbills had been torn down. It did not take long before they met in front of the jail. As far as they could tell, there was not one handbill still posted except for a couple that had been placed in the windows of businesses. They wondered if those just might disappear before the day was over.

Charlie walked into the jail with his brothers following. He turned a grim face to them and said, "Those hoodlums must think I'm foolin'. Well, they got 'nother think comin'. If ya see anybody who looks like they're drunk 'r are causin' trouble, bring 'em ta the jail an' lock 'em up.

I'd suggest that ya don't be goin' around by yourself. One of ya needs ta go back to the house an' git started doin' some things there an' the other two of ya stay together."

Tearing down of the handbills was just another step in the growing animosity between the Witwer brothers and the local hoodlums. For the next few weeks, Charlie and two of the brothers walked the streets, making themselves visible all day and late into the evening, watching for anyone causing trouble. Charlie wanted everyone to know that he was going to make the streets safe for the townspeople and any visitors that came to Hillview.

It was not long before they started to make use of one or more of the jail cells on a regular basis. Sometimes it was a local fellow or two, and occasionally it was a fellow from one of the surrounding towns. Charlie was usually the one that spent the night on the old cot in the jail when they kept someone overnight to sleep off the liquor. On those nights, he had to get the potbellied stove full of wood or coal and get a good fire going. He pulled his cot close to the stove so he could at least be a little bit warm. Charlie was not concerned about who was in the cells or whether or not they were keeping warm. He thought maybe a night in a cold jail cell would make an impression on the occupants, but there seemed to be no end to the amount of trouble they could cause.

Sometimes, if the occupants of the cell had not had enough to drink to make them go to sleep, there was more yelling going on than there was sleeping. Yelling at them to keep quiet did not have any effect on them so Charlie would spend a sleepless night. As the weeks passed and it got close to Christmas, there did not seem to be quite as many trouble-makers roaming around. Charlie was not sure if they were beginning to make a little progress, or if the weather was just too cold for anyone to be out causing trouble.

CHAPTER 20

Christmas Back Home in Missouri

Charlie told Mayor Coates that he and his brothers were going to go back to Mexico for Christmas, but they would not be gone much more than twenty-four hours. They had not told anyone else they were leaving, hoping that if the word did not get around, things would be quiet while they were gone. Charlie had worked almost every day, and the other three brothers had not taken much time off. They were all ready for a break from the daily stress.

On Christmas Eve, the four brothers each packed a small bag and hopped on the last train going through Hillview headed to Mexico. They were anxious to see the family. Charlie was most anxious to see Lucy. As they walked to the train station, all Dick could talk about was getting back to see if Liz was still his girl. Ernest and Jim were just happy to be going home for Christmas. They knew their mother, Nancy, and Lucy would have a table full of food for them the next day, and they looked forward to seeing their dad, Jacob. After a while, even Mrs. Greene's cooking got tiresome, although it was better than what they cooked at home. Most of the time what they cooked was wild rabbit and a can of pork and beans. Just thinking about what would be on the table on Christmas day made their mouths water.

The brothers thought they might get to see their little brother Harry if he did not run off to some friend's house, and their other brother Frank, who had moved to Springfield, Illinois, along with his wife Ethel. Neither Jim nor Ernest had been in contact with the wives they had left behind since they moved to Hillview. Nancy was not happy about that situation and hoped Charlie would try to change their minds. She wanted little Glenn to see his father, Ernest. Charlie had tried talking to Ernest and Jim before they left Hillview but had no success in changing their minds. They knew their mother would be thinking about her only daughter, Rose, who had moved to California some years before.

Family gatherings were always a joyous time in the Witwer household. Tonight each of the brothers had a few gifts stuffed in their bag to put under the Christmas tree. They were hoping their dad had cut a tree and that Lucy and their mother had decorated it.

Charlie had taken a lot of time to try to find something special for Lucy. He knew he had left her behind several weeks before and had a lot of making up to do. He had made special trip to White Hall to find a silver wedding band, and he sure hoped it fit her finger.

CHAPTER 21

The Family Gathering

Jacob and Nancy Witwer had been married for thirty-four years when Charlie married Lucy. Jacob "Jake" was forty-five years old when he married Nancy, who was twenty-two years old at the time of their marriage. Jacob was born in Harrisburg, Pennsylvania, and Nancy, half Cherokee Indian, was born in Arkansas. Jake had filled the minds of his children with many stories about fighting in the Civil War, and they begged him to repeat them over and over. He was proud that he had met Abraham Lincoln during the war. During his lifetime, he had driven a mule train, worked on the railroad, cut railroad ties, was a saddle and harness maker, a lumberjack, and did farm work. He was a hard worker and taught his boys to be hard workers. He passed on many of the skills he had learned to his sons. Growing up in the Pennsylvania Dutch countryside, he had learned to speak German but never taught the language to his children.

Nancy was half Cherokee Indian and passed on those physical Indian characteristics to a few of her sons, particularly Charlie. Nancy tried to teach her children to be tolerant of other people. She knew from experience what it was like to be discriminated against. An ugly incident occurred at school when she was seven years old, and it was one she never forgot. When she was in school, she was quite often taunted because she was half Cherokee Indian. One day, someone put horse manure in her lunch pail. That was the last day Nancy attended school. When her father heard what had happened, he was quick to decide that he was not going to send her back to school to be subjected to that kind of treatment. Her mother, who was a full-blooded Cherokee, taught her at home after that incident. She taught Nancy to speak some of the Cherokee language. When Nancy was infuriated with Jake, she would speak to him angrily in Cherokee—which may not have been words she would have spoken in English!

As the brothers hurried up the sidewalk that Christmas Eve, they were so excited they did not feel the wind whistling around them. They saw that every lamp was on in the house and Lucy, with the curtain pulled back, was looking out the front window. As they burst through the door into the front room, it was a cheerful scene—everyone laughing and talking at the same time. Nancy and Lucy had kept supper warm on the stove. After the hugs and backslapping was over, it did not take the brothers long to fill their plates and gobble up every morsel. Mrs. Greene's cooking was good but not as good as Lucy's and Nancy's. After all of them had eaten until they were stuffed, they sat around the potbellied stove in the front room. The stove was red hot and soon everyone's cheeks were rosy and eyelids were getting heavy. Jake was full of questions about what had been going on in Hillview. Nancy was more concerned about whether they were getting enough to eat. It was hard to get a word in with all of the chatter, so Lucy sat quietly with her chair close to Charlie's chair and her hand resting on his leg.

When the conversation came to a lull, Charlie looked at Lucy. Even with her housedress hanging loose, he could see that it would not be too long before the baby would be born. Looking at her, he said, "We got ta git ya ta Hillview. I think its time fer ya ta go back with us. I talked to Doc Garrison, and he said he'd be happy ta take care o' ya when the baby comes."

Lucy's face broke into a big grin and tears of happiness immediately filled her eyes. "That's the best Christmas gift I could git."

Charlie looked at Jacob and Nancy and said, "If this thing works out in Hillview, I think ya might want ta consider comin' ta live with us. Lucy'll be havin' ya a grandbaby."

Jake looked over at Nancy as she sat crocheting what looked like a baby blanket. Nancy did not say anything, but just nodded her head. Jacob looked around at his sons and said, "Well, when the weather gits warm, we just might do that."

Christmas morning was like old times. There never were many presents under the tree, but everyone had presents this year. Big tears rolled down Lucy's cheeks as she opened the box Charlie gave her and saw the silver wedding band. It was a little tight on her finger, but she assured Charlie that once the baby was born, it would be just perfect. Charlie was a little bit embarrassed at the fuss Lucy was making, but Nancy knew he was quite proud that he could make Lucy so happy.

As Christmas day ended, Lucy started packing her few belongings, getting ready to leave with Charlie and his brothers. She was so excited to be going with Charlie, her hands shook as she tried to pack her clothes. She knew she would miss Jacob and Nancy, and even Harry, but she yearned to be in Hillview with Charlie. She felt that her baby would be born within the month, and she wanted to be with Charlie for the birth.

Lucy had been hoping Dick would marry her sister, Liz, and then Liz could join the household in Hillview. That was something Lucy could look forward to. Living with the four brothers without another woman for company might be a challenge. She just knew life would be more pleasant if she had Liz with her. She knew Dick and Liz were sweet on each other, but she wondered if Dick would make a good husband. He had proposed to Liz late in the afternoon Christmas day, but Lucy wondered if he really wanted to marry Liz, or if he just had a little too much to drink. Dick promised he would come back to Mexico before long so he and Liz could get married.

As they ate Christmas leftovers in the early evening, they each knew it was about time for the brothers and Lucy to leave. It was a particularly hard time for Jacob and Nancy. The time had passed swiftly, and now Lucy was going to be leaving too. Charlie said they needed to get to the train station so they did not miss the last train headed to Hillview. It was hard to get Lucy's coat around her but they bundled her up so she would not get cold. Her bag was so heavy she could not lift it so Dick grabbed it along with his small bag. They said their solemn good-byes to Jacob and Nancy. Jacob and Nancy knew that Lucy belonged in Hillview with Charlie, but they were sad to see her leave with their boys. Nancy and Lucy stood clinging to each other, neither wanting to let go.

Train depot in Hillview, Illinois

Chapter 22

Slick's Demise

It was late when the train arrived in Hillview. They walked to the house, and Lucy was exhausted. She was not too tired to look around as they walked into the house, though. She looked around with a slight bit of disgust before saying, "All of ya better stay outta my way fer the next few days. This place looks like a pigpen. I cain't be havin' my baby born in a place like this."

Jim started to protest with a string of excuses, but after catching a glimpse of Charlie's face, decided it was best if he just got some wood to start a fire in the potbellied stove. The house was cold and everybody was tired. Dick and Ernest headed down the hall dropping Lucy's bag in her and Charlie's bedroom, and then made themselves scarce.

The next few days were quiet around the Witwer household—as long as they all stayed out of Lucy's way. She worked on getting the house cleaned up, and she did not want to be bothered with any of them unless they were going to help her. She barely stopped working long enough to cook anything for them to eat. Charlie spent all of his time trying to keep the peace around town. There had not been any major disturbances, just minor skirmishes that Charlie was able to keep under control.

Lucy made trips to Patterson's Store, buying material to make curtains and to purchase other household items. She worked hard at trying to make the house livable. Charlie was glad he had saved a little money. Lucy was not happy with the condition of the house and did not hesitate to make her feelings known. He thought it best to not say much about what she was spending and get her all riled up. If any of them hung around the house very long, she would start giving them orders about what they could do to help. Jim, Ernest, and Dick tried to spend as much time trapping and hunting as they could whenever Charlie did not want them patrolling the town. He did tell them that one of them had to stay around the house for a little while each day and help Lucy get the house the way she wanted it. They grumbled when Charlie and Lucy could not hear them, but they did get some of the repairs done that had been put off.

In early January, pounding on the front door at about four in the morning awakened Jim, who was a light sleeper. He jumped out of bed and grabbed the kerosene lamp on the nightstand. He quickly lit it and headed for the front door. By this time everybody in the house except Charlie was awake and poking their heads out of their bedroom doors. As Jim cracked open the front door, the man standing on the porch said, "There's been a killing, and I need to talk to Marshal Charlie."

Jim opened the screen door and motioned for him to come in. "I'll git 'im up." About that time, Charlie staggered out of the bedroom in only his long underwear. Squinting in the dim light of the kerosene lamp, he recognized the man standing in the doorway as a switchman from the railroad.

"Did I hear ya right? Somebody got killed?"

"Yeah, we found a man torn to pieces on the railroad tracks and under the engine. The engineer said he saw a naked man who looked like he was blindfolded being pushed in front of the engine about a mile east of Hillview. It took him over a mile to get the freight train stopped. There ain't much left of whoever it was. Most of him is spread out along the track. The engineer went to the hotel and woke up the night clerk so he could use the phone in the lobby to call the mayor. The mayor said to get a hold of you, so the engineer told me to come and get you."

By this time, Charlie was jerking on his pants and suspenders and shoving his feet into his boots. He looked up and asked, "Has anybody called the coroner?" As he threw his coat on, he noticed that Lucy was up and standing in the bedroom doorway. "Go back ta bed. Ya don't need ta be gittin' up fer this."

By this time, Dick had his clothes on. "Charlie, I'm goin' with ya." Charlie just shook his head and said, "Okay, let's see what this is all 'bout. Jim and Ernest, stay home with Lucy. I don't want her here alone."

As they quickly walked down the street and approached the tracks, Charlie and Dick could see the engine standing idle with smoke and steam still coming out of the stack. They crossed the bridge over Hurricane Creek, walked around the front of the engine, and were stunned by what they saw. Caught in the cowcatcher on the front of the engine was an object that looked like someone's forearm. The engineer had a railroad lantern, which shed a yellow-orange light on the object in the cowcatcher. Dick walked up a bit closer to the hanging object so he could get a good look. He walked back to Charlie and said, "That is an arm an' it has a tattoo on it. I know who has a tattoo like that!"

Charlie frowned at Dick and said, "Ya sure 'bout that?"

"Yeah, I'm sure. A gambler called Slick has a tattoo just like that on his arm. He usually catches the train down here on weekends an' stirs up a card game over at the hotel. Suckers always show up with money. I played cards with 'im a couple a times an' figured out right away that he was too slick fer me. He usually plays 'til everybody's broke. Nobody seems ta know what his real name is 'r where he's from. I'll bet this is Slick. If it is, he won't be dealin' a fast deck anymore."

About that time, Mayor Coates walked up to Charlie. His first comments were "My God, what'll happen around here next? I called the deputy coroner. He said he'd get a coroner's jury together as soon as possible, and they would look over the body for signs of trauma. Not sure how he's going to do that from the looks of things."

Dick piped up and said, "They'll have ta put 'im back together first."

Charlie just glared at Dick and said, "Show a little respect. If ya kin find out who's been playin' cards, we just might figur' out fer sure if this is Slick and who done 'im in. Ya have any idea who was playin' cards?"

Mayor Coates responded, "I'm not for sure, but I think I saw Frank Patterson and a couple of others walk into the hotel last night. I think some card games go on in there."

Charlie looked at Dick and said, "Go over ta the hotel an' see if that desk clerk knows anythin' 'bout a card game goin' on last night. If he don't know, find out who was workin'. As soon as it gits light, we need ta start tryin' ta find out who was playin' cards. As soon as ya do that, go back ta the house an' tell Ernest an' Jim what's goin' on. Make sure Lucy's okay, an' then all o' ya git back ta town and see what ya can find out."

The engineer said, "We got to get that guy's remains off my cowcatcher and get the tracks back there cleaned up. I got to get this freight train rollin'."

Charlie said, "You ain't goin' nowhere 'til the coroner gits here. I was a railroad detective, an' I know how these things work. Ya should be makin' a report fer the railroad office fer yer own protection but you'll have ta wait 'til after the coroner gits here."

It was just breaking daylight when the deputy coroner arrived. He looked at the engineer and said, "What the hell happened?" As the engineer related the story, the deputy coroner made notes in his black binder that he always carried with him. After a quick survey of those standing around, he looked up and said, "Somebody call Doc Garrison. He needs to be here when we take that body part off the front of your cowcatcher. Has anybody looked under the train to see if there are any more parts of this person under there?"

Dick, who had not yet left, looked at the deputy corner and said, "Hell, that's yer job. I ain't gittin' under that train." When he glanced over at Charlie, who was glaring at him, he knew it was time for him to do what Charlie had told him to do and took off running. Charlie's glare spoke loud and clear.

The engineer was getting anxious because he knew the eastbound passenger train should be pulling through Hillview in about an hour. His freight train was on the main track, and there was no way the passenger train could get through. The last thing he needed was a train wreck, especially with a passenger train. The engineer looked at Charlie and said, "Charlie, we got to do something pretty quick, or we're goin' to have a hell of a mess. A passenger train is due in about an hour."

Charlie thought for a minute, looked at the engineer, and said, "Have yer switchman run down the tracks an' pull all the red switches. That other engineer oughta be smart enough ta figure out there's a problem. Mayor Coates, go ta the railroad station an' telegraph the Louisiana, Missouri, depot. Tell 'em ta stop that damn train 'r we'll have a bigger mess on our hands."

By this time, it was light enough to see people gathering on the depot platform waiting for the passenger train to come through. From the platform, you could not see the cowcatcher on the train or what was hanging on it. All of a sudden, a woman screamed and yelled, "What's hanging off the side of the train?"

Charlie looked at Mayor Coates and said, "We got ta git those people outta there now!"

Not waiting for Doc Garrison, the deputy coroner came around to the front of the engine with a large galvanized tub and some towels he had found in the train station. He was not sure why they were in the station but sure was glad to have them. He grabbed a towel and reached up on the cowcatcher and, with a little tug, managed to pull the arm out of the metal grates. He gingerly placed it in the galvanized tub. He put some towels over it, set it down by the edge of the railroad track and walked around to the south side of the engine toward the coal hopper. When he was about halfway past the coal hopper, he bent over with his hands on his knees and looked under it.

"My God. What a mess. Can someone help me get what's hanging down under this train? There's not much left of whoever it is. That tattoo may be the only thing we've got to identify him."

A few people had gathered around but nobody made a move to help. The mayor heard the coroner asking for help but figured nobody would volunteer for such a job, so he reluctantly walked around the train and proceeded to help retrieve the mutilated torso. After placing the remains in the tub and covering it once again, the deputy coroner pointed to the galvanized tub and said to Mayor Coates, "If you just keep an eye on this tub, I'll try to get together a coroner's jury. I know some of the people on the station platform who might be willing to be on the jury."

Mayor Coates was not sure his stomach was going to cooperate but he nodded his head and said, "Yes, but hurry up. My stomach is in an uproar, and I didn't expect to be standing out here this long. I'm freezing. We need to get this mess taken care of as soon as possible."

The engineer and Charlie huddled shoulder to shoulder in the cold morning light discussing what exactly had taken place and the possibility of moving the train up the track a little way. Mayor Coates had managed to get a telegraph message to the Louisiana Railroad Station, and they were able to stop the passenger train in Louisiana. Charlie turned to Mayor Coates and told him that he would watch the tub if he would send another telegraph to the Louisiana Station and advise them that the passenger train should wait about thirty minutes more before heading to Hillview. Charlie and the engineer had decided that the engineer and the switchman could take the train up the tracks, change the track's switch, and pull the freight train onto the siding. The mayor was more than happy to give up his assigned job of watching the tub of remains and took off for the telegraph office.

Dick had made a quick trip to the house and then stopped by the Phoenix Hotel to talk to the desk clerk. He ran over to Charlie and said, "I need ta talk ta ya where nobody can hear what I'm sayin'." Charlie and Dick walked around to the side of the train, away from the conductor and the townsfolk that were standing around trying to hear what was going on.

"Accordin' ta the desk clerk, there were at least three people besides Slick who he thought might o' been in the card game. He said there might o' even been more. Slick rented that room in the back o' the lobby last night. The one that has a big card table in it. Ya know, that one at the back end o' the hotel, near the back door. You'll never guess who two o' those people were!"

Charlie looked a little perturbed. "Dammit, Dick, who were they?"

"F. H. Patterson and Samuel Mundy, but he wouldn't tell me who the other one was that he saw go in. His excuse was that a lot o' people walked through the lobby an' out the back door. Said several people had been in the lobby earlier in the evenin', an' he couldn't say fer sure who they were 'r where they were goin'. He acted kind o' funny when I was talkin' ta 'im."

Charlie just scratched his chin. "When we git this mess cleaned up an' the trains rollin', I'll go see Patterson. I'm sure he'll tell me who else was in the game."

The deputy coroner took the tub into the railroad station where he had hastily gathered twelve people to act as a coroner's jury. Charlie was not sure how he had gathered twelve people together so quickly and so early in the morning, but he had more things to be concerned about. It was not long before the jury members walked out of the station, followed by the deputy coroner. He handed Charlie a handwritten statement, which simply stated that the coroner's jury had arrived at an "open verdict." Charlie knew a verdict written in that manner only meant that it could have been an accident or suicide, but in no way did the verdict indicate the possibility of murder.

Charlie read the statement and reread the statement. Anyone looking at Charlie could see his jaw clench and his brown eyes turn dark as he looked at the deputy coroner and said, "What the hell's goin' on here? You know damn well this guy was shoved in front o' the train. You heard what the engineer said."

The coroner replied, "That's the verdict the jury came up with. We've had enough bad publicity in Hillview, and we don't want a bunch of newspaper people coming over here and giving Hillview a worse name than it already has. If those remains are that gambler Slick, and it appears that they are because of that tattoo, he's been comin' to Hillview and cheatin' people out of their money. No great loss. My jury and I agreed that this was the best thing to do. If you don't like it, Charlie, and you can prove it was murder and who did it, then you have the authority as an officer of the law to arrest them and charge them with the crime. Until you can do that, the jury's findings hold."

The coroner's short speech did nothing more than make Charlie even madder. He was furious! He thought to himself that justice was not important to some of these townsfolk. Their justification to cover up a murder was unacceptable to Charlie, no matter what they thought about the person. And, trying to hide a murder was not going to make the streets of Hillview any safer.

Dick watched the confrontation between the coroner and Charlie. Dick knew Charlie was a man who valued fairness. He had never seen such anger and disappointment displayed on Charlie's face. Dick walked quietly over to Charlie and touched him on the arm. "Come on, Charlie. Let's go on back home an' see if we can git somethin' ta eat. I know Lucy cooked up breakfast fer Ernest and Jim. She probably kept something warm fer us."

As they walked over the bridge and up the hill to the house, Charlie did not utter a word. Dick knew from experience that it was a good idea to leave Charlie to his thoughts and for him to keep his mouth shut.

Jim had run down to the railroad station for a few minutes to see what was going on but had gotten back to the house ahead of Charlie and Dick. He had told Lucy and Ernest what had happened. Lucy had baked biscuits, made a pan of gravy, and had another pot of coffee made. They were all sitting on the stove keeping warm for Charlie to come home. Dick had grabbed a biscuit when he had run back to the house earlier, but she knew he would still be hungry. She looked out of the window and saw Charlie and Dick striding swiftly toward the house. Charlie's face was set in a scowl, and he was walking so fast Dick almost had to run to keep up with him. This was not a good sign.

She poured four cups of coffee and put the biscuits and gravy on the table but did not wait for Charlie and Dick to walk through the front door. She simply went to her bedroom and closed the door. She thought she might even slip out the back door and go to Patterson's store. She got pretty tired walking these days, and her coat did not cover her middle all the way anymore, but from the look on

Charlie's face, Lucy knew it was best that she let the four brothers hash this thing out.

As Charlie and Dick came through the door, Jim and Ernest sat down at the table and waited for them to sit down. For several minutes after everyone sat down, the only sound was the scraping of their forks on their plates. Jim was the first one to speak out. "I bet my best coon dog it was those damn thugs that shoved Slick under the train."

Ernest nodded his head and said, "You're probably right, but how we goin' ta prove it?"

Charlie still did not say anything and for a few minutes did nothing more than stare at his coffee cup. He looked up from his cup and said, "I'm goin' down ta the post office in a few minutes. Patterson will be there, an' I'm sure he'll tell me who was in that card game. Ernest, after ya finish eatin', I want ya ta go ta Mrs. Greene's Restaurant, and see what kind o' information you can pick up. Jim, go down ta the pool hall an' see what's goin' on there. Dick, go hang around a couple saloons an' see what ya can find out but don't be drinkin' any liquor. All o' ya just hang around an' see if ya can hear anythin' that might give us a clue. I don't think this was an accident, an' I sure don't think it was a suicide. I think this was a murder no matter what that coroner's jury says. I'm not sure these people want their town cleaned up."

They all nodded at Charlie, grabbed another biscuit to eat on the way, and took off. It was almost noon and the sun was high in the sky, but it was a cold January morning. As they crossed the bridge and railroad track, they headed to the downtown area. They could see several people hanging around the front of Patterson's store, and they knew what the topic of conversation was.

Before noon, both the passenger train and the freight train were on their way to their destinations. The deputy coroner had called the funeral home in Whitehall, and they were sending a hearse to pick up the remains. The coroner advised the funeral director that he was not aware of the identity of the remains, but assured him that if no one came to claim the body, the town of Hillview would pick up a reasonable amount for the burial. He hinted to the funeral director to keep this as quiet as he could.

CHAPTER 23

The Investigation

Charlie walked quickly to Patterson's store. It was early so there were not many people in the aisles. He saw Mr. Patterson sorting some papers and asked if he had any mail in his box.

Patterson said, "Your box is empty right now. The mail will be here in an hour or so. Check with me after that."

Charlie noticed that Mr. Patterson turned his head and kept his eyes away from Charlie's penetrating stare. "There was a card game at the hotel last night. Were ya in that card game?

"Yes, I was, but I left early because I lost my stake and went home."

"I'm sure ya know by now, somebody got run over by the train last night. There wasn't much left o' the body, but we could see a tattoo on a piece o' his arm that we found. Some people said there's been a gambler come through here with the same tattoo, an' his name was Slick. Know anythin' 'bout that?" Mr. Patterson simply shook his head.

"Who else was in the game?"

As Mr. Patterson answered, he continued shuffling papers and did not look directly at Charlie. "Mr. Mundy and three other guys who I didn't know."

Charlie felt that Mr. Patterson knew more than what he was willing to talk about. Charlie had always trusted Mr.

Patterson but thought maybe he was not telling everything he knew because he was afraid his wife might disapprove of his gambling. Or, had he been threatened if he talked to anyone? Charlie felt that putting pressure on Mr. Patterson would not accomplish anything right then. Maybe after things calmed down in a day or two, Mr. Patterson would be more willing to talk.

Jim, Ernest, nor Dick had any luck in getting information that day either. It seemed as though nobody had any information or wanted to talk to them about what might have occurred during the night.

For the next few days, there was an unusual stillness throughout Hillview. It seemed as though people were staying close to home, and those who were out were not saying much. Even Mrs. Greene's Restaurant had fewer customers. Jim, Ernest, nor Dick had been able to find out anything as they mingled with the townspeople. They made some inquiries, but no one seemed to know anything. Even more surprising was the fact that there was no inquiry from anyone about a missing person or about Slick.

Dick was making his rounds in an official capacity one afternoon and was getting rather bored. The streets were quiet and he was cold, so he decided to stop in one of the saloons to have a drink. Charlie did not care if he went into a saloon when he was working, but he frowned on Dick having anything to drink. Dick thought it would not hurt this one time, and he was sure Charlie was going to be at home. As Dick stood around the bar, one of the young men at the end of the bar by the nickname of Butch was talking rather loudly. Butch was a tall, lanky young man who was often seen with Clarence "Bum" Deeds and Isom Leonard. It was well known around Hillview that Butch liked to play poker but was not very good at the game. Butch took a pocket watch out of his pocket, and a couple of the other young men were looking at it. There was a large clock on the wall above the mirror behind the bar, so they did not need to look at the pocket watch for the time. Dick walked to the end of the bar and said, "What time do ya got?"

It was late in the afternoon, and there was a good chance that Butch had already had quite a bit to drink. Before he recognized who was talking to him, he raised the gold watch and flipped open the case with a flourish. He turned and started to answer. When he saw Dick, he glared at him.

"Can't you see the damn clock behind the bar?"

Dick replied, "Well, I just wasn't sure that was the right time, an' I saw ya had yer pocket watch out. Where'd ya come across a fancy watch like that?"

Butch quickly put the watch in his pocket and turned his back on Dick. "It's none of your damn business. Just leave me alone."

Dick walked back to where his drink was sitting and began to sip it slowly, staring down at Butch. Dick decided to see how far he could push him. In a loud voice, so that everyone in the bar could hear, he looked at Butch and said, "I knew a guy who had a watch zactly like that one. He's dead now, but when he was alive, he was a hell of a poker player. They called 'im Slick. Someone said you were playin' poker with 'im the night he died. Anythin' ta that?"

Butch grabbed the shot glass and tossed the liquor down his throat. He shuffled unsteadily across the gritty floor and started toward the coat rack. As he walked by Dick he said, "You ain't got nothin' on me, and 'til you do, you leave me alone."

Dick casually replied, "We'll see."

Dick was not sure if Charlie was home, but he ran all the way to the house. He wanted to find him as quickly as he could. He busted through the door hollering for Charlie. Charlie was in the kitchen with Jim and Ernest. They had just gotten home and were getting a cup coffee.

"Charlie, I know who killed Slick, or at least one o' the killers." Dick was excited and out of breath, so it took several minutes for him to calm down and tell what had happened in the saloon.

The three brothers sat staring at Dick as he told his story and were silent for what seemed like an eternity to Dick. He was just sure they would be as excited as he was. Jim finally said, "Dick, I'm sure yer right, but there ain't no way ta prove that watch belonged ta Slick."

Ernest said, "He ain't the first guy that got shoved in front of a train in Hillview, an' the coroner an' his jury always come up with the same verdict—an open verdict. That gang has got this town terrified ta the point where the people won't cooperate with the law fer fear o' meetin' with the same fate that Slick met up with. Charlie, we've been here fer over two months an' we ain't accomplished a damn thing when it comes ta gettin' rid of these gangs or stoppin' the trouble they cause."

Charlie was infuriated at the whole situation but said, "Well, it may be hard ta prove who killed Slick even if you're right, Dick. Our job is ta protect the citizens of Hillview, an' not some tin horn gambler from who-knows-where. We're lawmen an' we have ta operate within the law."

The brothers were shocked at what Charlie said. Charlie noticed the surprise on their faces and added, "Sooner or later, these troublemakers will make mistakes, an' when they do, we'll take 'em in, one by one, an' it'll be for more than overnight."

CHAPTER 24

The Birth of Everett Eugene

In the early morning hours of January 14, 1914, the wind was howling through the thin panes of the bedroom window as the sleet made pecking sounds on it. They had been lucky so far that winter and had not had much sleet or snow. Lucy had been uncomfortable during the late afternoon and evening hours with pains and felt that her baby was going to be born sometime soon. She had not said anything to Charlie but wished Nancy was with her. It was so cold that everyone had gone to bed early trying to keep warm in the feather beds. She knew they had plenty of firewood and was thankful for that. Charlie lay sound asleep beside her, snoring as usual.

The last three weeks since Charlie brought her to Hillview had not been easy ones for Lucy as she tried to get the house cleaned and curtains up to the windows, along with cooking for four men. They ate so much she thought they must have been making up for the time before she came to cook for them. She sent one of the brothers to Patterson's nearly every day to buy supplies or groceries. Sometimes she would go with them if they took the Model T. She was always too tired to walk very far. Every night she fell into bed exhausted from the day's chores. Even as exhausted as she was, she could not find a comfortable position and kept tossing and turning. She was not afraid the tossing and turning would wake Charlie since it would take a freight train running through the middle of the house to wake him.

When the pains started getting more intense and closer together, she knew it was time to wake Charlie and to get one of the others to go for the doctor. She poked Charlie trying to rouse him, but all he did was grunt and roll over. After a couple more times of poking and getting just more grunts, she decided it would be easier to wake up Jim. She hated to crawl out of the feather mattress and covers and walk on the cold floor, but she knew it was time

The feather mattress was a special thing Charlie had bought for her after she came to Hillview. He had sent Dick to White Hall to pick out the best mattress and pillows he could find so that Lucy would be more comfortable as her pregnancy progressed. As she crawled out of bed, heavy with the weight of the baby, she padded slowly across the hall to Jim's room. The heavy woolen socks she wore to bed every cold night helped little against the wooden floors that were as cold as ice. Standing in her nightgown with the pains gripping her body, she shook Jim and called his name. Jim immediately sat straight up in bed and said, "What's goin' on? What's wrong?"

The fire had not been stoked in the potbellied stove the night before, and the house was very cold. The wind was blowing outside, and it seemed like the sleety snow hitting the windows was getting louder. Even the inside of the windowpanes were etched with frost. The cold air blowing in around the windowsills made the curtains look like they were doing a dance. They had tried to stuff rags around some of the worst windows, but even those provided little relief on a night like this.

As Lucy replied, you could almost see her breath. "I'm havin' awful pains, an' I think I'm about ta have this baby. You need ta git Charlie awake, and then go git Doc Garrison. Wake up Ernest 'r Dick an' have 'im git a fire goin'."

About that time, Ernest came into the room holding a kerosene lamp. "What's goin' on?"

"Lucy is 'bout ta have this baby. We need ta go git Doc Garrison an' git a fire goin' ta warm this place up. Its freezin' in here. Go wake Charlie up. He needs ta be awake when he becomes a dad."

All the brothers had been around as their mother had given birth to each one of the children, so they did not panic but knew they needed to get the doctor as soon as possible. Being in the same house when a baby was born was one thing, but they did not want to be helping with the birth of Lucy's baby. By this time, Dick came down the hall and figured out what the commotion was about once he saw the look on Lucy's face. He immediately turned into Charlie's room. He walked over to the bed and gave Charlie a good shake to get him awake.

Charlie sat straight up in bed and swung his legs over the bed frame. He looked over to see that Lucy was not on her side. "Where's Lucy?"

"Lucy said she's havin' this baby pretty soon an' somebody needs ta git Dr. Garrison. I think Ernest 'r Jim is gittin' ready ta go, but ya need ta git up an' take care o' Lucy. She's sitting on a chair in Jim's room. Go help her git back ta bed. She's freezin' an' she's havin' pains."

Ernest put on everything he could find to keep warm and trudged onto the ice-covered porch. He could tell that the streets were slick from the way they glistened and knew that it would be a slow trip. It was too cold to try to start the Model T, and he knew that it would take more time than if he just walked. Maybe Doc Garrison would drive his car back to the house.

Charlie helped Lucy get back in bed and then got dressed. Charlie had been at home when his mother had given birth to the rest of the children in the family, but this was different. This was Lucy, and this was his baby that was about to be born! He did not want to act nervous in front of Lucy or his brothers, but his stomach was churning and doing flip-flops. His heart was beating so loud and fast, he could hear it in his ears. Maybe he needed a good hot cup of coffee—or something even stronger! He had to get Lucy back to bed first.

Jim spent his time getting the fire going in the potbellied stove. He sent Dick to the woodpile in the back and told him to stack a lot on the back porch so they would have plenty. This storm might not let up, and it would be better to get the wood into the house so it could dry. By daybreak, the house had gotten warmer, but the wind was still howling, and the sleet continued to peck on the windows. Charlie was getting more nervous as Lucy's pains seemed to be getting closer together and harder each time she had one. He wondered if Ernest was going to get back with the doctor before this baby was born.

It was not long before the front door flew open, and Ernest and Doc Garrison came rushing in with a blast of cold air. Doc had his little black bag with him. Just seeing him and that little black bag made Charlie feel a whole lot better. The doctor had not had much sleep when Ernest came banging on his door. He had been at the Hanover's house most of the evening and late into the night trying to take care of Mr. Hanover after he had nearly cut his foot off with an ax. The weather was terrible and he was tired, but he had promised Charlie he would be with Lucy for the birth of their first child.

Doc Garrison walked down the hall to the bedroom and saw Charlie, Jim, and Dick looking at Lucy with helpless expressions on their faces. It did not take long to figure out that nobody was going to be of any help, but he started giving orders immediately.

"One of you get a couple of pans of water heated on the stove, and one of you bring me some clean towels. Make sure we have a pan of hot water going all of the time, and keep that fire going so it stays warm in here. Then go in the kitchen and sit down. I don't think Lucy or I need any of you in here getting in our way when this baby starts coming."

None of them hesitated. Without a word, they just turned and quickly walked down the hall to the kitchen. Dick got a couple of big pots out and filed them with water. He had to get the cook stove going so they could heat the water. Jim went back to keeping the fire going in the potbellied stove in the living room. On his way, he told Ernest to find some towels and take them to Doc Garrison. Fortunately, Charlie did not have a job to do; he was doing just about all he could do just to stay calm. None of the brothers said much, but they were all thinking the same thing—Charlie is going to be a dad!

After Jim, Ernest, and Dick had done what Doc Garrison told them to do, they were ready to start thinking about something to eat. Lucy was having a baby, but that did not keep them from wanting breakfast. Jim busied himself making a pot of strong coffee and tried to find some leftover biscuits and a jar of jelly. They had gotten used to Lucy fixing their breakfast, but that was not going to happen today, or for the next few days. About the only thing to be heard was the sound of the coffeepot as it percolated, punctuated by the sound of the sleet pecking against the window in a rhythmic pattern. Every few minutes they could hear a moan and the soothing voice of Doc Garrison. Charlie paced back and forth from the kitchen to the living room while the other three pulled up chairs at the kitchen table.

Dick grinned at Charlie and said, "Here's a cup a strong coffee, Charlie. Maybe it'll settle yer nerves. Yer makin' us nervous with all that pacin' yer doin'. Have ya picked out a name yet? Maybe ya should name 'im Dick after me if it's a boy."

Charlie stopped his pacing and looked at his brothers. He did not want to look like he was nervous, so he grabbed a chair and sat down.

"I'm goin' ta let Lucy name the baby. Women do a better job at that. But I sure won't let 'er name 'im after you!"

Charlie could not sit still and started pacing again. The other three brothers sat at the kitchen table sipping their coffee and chewing on the cold leftover biscuits. At least the jelly made them taste a little better. Every so often, they would hear Lucy let out a yell, followed, once again, by the soothing murmurings of Doc Garrison. All of a sudden, Charlie stopped pacing to listen carefully. He thought he heard the sound of a baby crying, but soon discovered it was only the sound of one of the dogs yelping in the back yard. Charlie went back to his pacing and the minutes seemed to stand still. Suddenly a grin broke out across Dick's face and he jumped up. "Did you hear that? I think ya just became a dad, Charlie. Ya keep calling this baby a 'him.' I'll bet ya a buck it's a girl."

Charlie reached in his pocket, pulled out a five-dollar bill, put it on the table, and said over his shoulder as he walked out of the kitchen, "How confident are ya?"

Dick just laughed as he pulled a five-dollar bill from his pocket and said, "This is goin' ta be the easiest five bucks I ever made."

As Charlie headed down the hallway, he met Doc Garrison coming out of the bedroom. "Charlie, would you like to meet yer son?"

Charlie was speechless at first, and then he yelled back at Dick and said, "Don't ya touch those five dollar bills 'cause ya just lost a bet. I got me a son." Charlie looked at Doc Garrison, "Is Lucy okay?"

"I think they'll both be just fine. The baby is a little on the small side, but I know that Lucy will take good care of him. I'm going to finish a few things with Lucy. Just give me a couple of minutes to get cleaned up, and I'll head for home. I'm tired. You fellas can clean up this room, and you can come get me if there's any trouble."

When Doc Garrison walked out of the room a short while later, Charlie walked over to the bed, looked down at Lucy with as big a grin on his face as Lucy had ever seen. "From now on, I guess we'll have ta call ya 'Mom.'"

It had been a long night for Lucy, but the look on her face as she peered down at her baby son was one that Charlie would never forget. As she looked up at Charlie, she gave him a loving smile and said, "That's just fine with me, Dad. Do ya want ta hold yer son, Dad?"

As Charlie sat down on the edge of the bed, the springs squeaked loudly, which made them both grin. As he took the baby from Lucy's arms he said, "He ain't very big, is he?"

"No, but I'll fatten 'im up in no time. We never did talk much 'bout names, but I'd like ta name him Everett Eugene, if that's okay?"

"I like that name. Ya can name 'im whatever ya want just so ya don't name 'im Dick!" Lucy looked at him quizzically and wondered why Charlie had said that but did not ask.

Charlie carefully handed Everett Eugene back to Lucy and went back to the kitchen. "Well, ya three just became uncles. We got ta let Lucy rest. She's had a hard night. An' I don't want ya botherin' 'er fer a few days. She needs ta rest an' git 'er strength back. All she needs ta be doin' is takin' care of Everett Eugene."

"Everett Eugene!" the three brothers said in unison. "Where'd that name come from?"

"That's what Lucy wants ta name our baby, so his name is goin' ta be Everett Eugene. Don't ya be askin' Lucy where that name came from. It don't matter—that's his name!"

Ernest pulled out four cigars from his pocket and handed one to Charlie, Jim, and Dick. "I been savin' these fer a special occasion, an' I cain't rightly think of anythin' more special than this. Congratulations, Pop. You done a good job."

"Lucy an' the boy will be callin' me Dad, an' the three o' ya can keep on callin' me Charlie. Now, why don't ya go on about yer business? Somebody needs ta check down at the jail. With this weather, I don't think there'll be anything goin' on today but somebody needs ta be there. Ya other two can haul in some more firewood an' git some chores done 'round here. Somebody's got ta cook us somthin' ta eat. Too bad outside ta be doin' anythin' out there. I'm goin' ta stay right here an' make sure Lucy's okay."

By the next day, the sun came out bright in the clear, blue sky. It was still bitterly cold, and the yard was full of branches that had been snapped by the ice, but just seeing the sun made everyone feel happier. It was a joyous time in the Witwer household. Another generation was born!

The next few days passed quickly. Lucy rested a few days and spent her time taking care of Everett Eugene. Living with four men and a baby did not afford her the luxury of lying in bed long, though. She could hear them arguing about who had to do the cooking and then complaining about what was cooked.

Lucy hoped Dick and Liz would get married soon so Liz could move in and help with some of the cooking and cleaning. She also would welcome the company of a female, especially her sister. Before Everett Eugene was born, she rarely had any free time. Now her days fell into a cycle of changing Everett Eugene's diapers, nursing him, bathing him, rocking him, cleaning the house, and cooking three meals a day—without much help from the male population in the household.

Everett Eugene Witwer
born January 14, 1914; died July 30, 1914

Chapter 25

Good-Bye, Everett Eugene

Everett Eugene did not thrive in the coming months. He kept very little of Lucy's milk down and did not gain weight, as he should have. Doc Garrison tried a variety of remedies, but nothing seemed to help. Lucy would sit for hours in the rocking chair holding her son, humming a song, rocking back and forth, as if she could rock him to health. Sometimes in the middle of the night, Charlie would hear the floor creaking with the sound of the rocking chair rocking back and forth. He knew that Lucy would have pulled the rocker close to the potbellied stove as she rocked Everett Eugene. Often when he went to check on her, he would see the tracks of tears on her face as she glanced up at him. Neither of them knew what words to say to comfort the other.

In July, when Everett Eugene was six months old, Dick and Liz got married. Liz moved into the house with the rest of the family in Hillview. Liz had been waiting in Mexico since Christmas when Dick had proposed to her. She thought he was never going to come back to get her. Her parents objected strenuously to the marriage, but she was as determined to marry Dick, as Lucy had been to marry Charlie. She was looking forward to being with Lucy and Everett Eugene, and Lucy certainly was glad to have her part of the household.

Liz was able to take on many of the chores as Lucy spent more and more time in that rocking chair with

Everett Eugene. As time passed, Everett Eugene became weaker and weaker. He cried very little and spent most of his hours sleeping, much of them in Lucy's arms. After sponging him off one afternoon at the end of July, Lucy rocked him a little and put him in his cradle for a nap. That was the last time she saw her son alive. When she went to check on him a short while later, Everett Eugene had drawn his last breath.

There were no words to describe Lucy's feelings as she saw that small lifeless body in the cradle. She let out a scream, which brought Liz running to the bedroom. There she found Lucy clutching Everett Eugene and sobbing uncontrollably. Liz ran to the back door to holler for Jim to tell him to go find Charlie.

Lucy spent her days and nights wondering why her baby had died when she had tried so hard to take care of him, but no one, not even Doc Garrison, had an answer for her. Charlie tried hard not to show the pain he was feeling, but everybody knew the turmoil that was going on inside. He had lost his firstborn son. Each of his brothers felt the loss too. They had lost their nephew. Liz did her best to console Lucy and to keep up with the household chores. Liz had only been with Lucy for a couple of weeks, but she too had grown to love little Everett Eugene.

The funeral services were conducted for Everett Eugene Witwer by Rev. W. H. McGhee of White Hall and were held in the White Hall Baptist Church. The burial took place in Martin's Cemetery, east of White Hall. The Witwer household was a solemn place for weeks after the death of Everett Eugene. Lucy looked tired and pale and was inconsolable. She seemed to go about her daily chores in a trance and said very little unless someone spoke directly to her. Charlie could hear her sobbing night after night but did not know what to do.

After Everett Eugene's funeral, Rev. McGhee visited the Witwer household on several occasions and spent many hours with Lucy trying to help her through the grieving process. He suggested to her that she might get comfort by attending the Baptist church in Hillview. At first, Lucy was somewhat reluctant because she knew none of the Witwer brothers went into a church unless it was for a funeral. She remembered that on a few occasions in Mexico, Ernest had attended Sunday services but knew that Charlie did not think much of going to church. Both she and Liz had attended Sunday services as they were growing up, only because their father had insisted they accompany him and their mother. Even though Charlie felt the pain of his son's death, he did not want any part of church. When Lucy mentioned it to him a few times, he told Lucy he had no objection if she went but not to keep asking him to go.

As the weeks passed and there was no relief from the despair that seemed to be locked inside Lucy's heart, Liz asked her if she would like to attend Sunday services with her at the Baptist church that was not far from their house. When Charlie heard about this, knowing that Ernest had occasionally gone to church, he asked Ernest if he would accompany Lucy and Liz. Ernest agreed without hesitation. None of them had many church clothes, but the three of them climbed the steps as the first hymn was starting one Sunday morning and slid into the back pew. Lucy was overwhelmed, even on that first Sunday, at how friendly and accepting the people were. She had become somewhat of a recluse after the death of Everett Eugene and had not realized how much she missed seeing people. After a few weeks, going to church on Sunday morning became an important part of their week, and Lucy's spirit gradually returned. Even Liz and Ernest seemed to be happier as they made friends with those who attended church. Occasionally, all three of them even attended the Wednesday night prayer service. The sadness that had filled the Witwer household lifted gradually, and there was no one more thankful than

Charlie. His heart started to heal as he saw Lucy begin to smile once again.

Edwards for Sheriff!

To Greene County Democrats:

ON WEDNESDAY, Sept. 9th, you will nominate a candidate for sheriff. Mr. Democrat, I want to be that candidate. Since I cannot be elected unless I am nominated, I earnestly urge all my friends to be at the polls primary day and bring out the full vote. Remember this, if you have my candidacy at heart and really wish to aid me, it must be on Wednesday. Sept. 9th. I am in this race to win and by your vote and influence, I will win.

I have made as thorough a campaign as possible, but the time has been entirely too short for me to see every voter personally, so if I have missed you in my rapid canvass of the county, I trust and believe you will take my candidacy under advisement and consider me favorably. Make inquiries of your friends and neighbors who know me personally, who know me as a man and a citizen, and then vote accordingly. My life is an open book, I will abide by the verdict of those who know me. I will appreciate your vote and good will and the good will of your friends.

Sincerely yours,

Jesse R. Edwards.

Jesse Edwards, appointed sheriff January 2, 1915

Witwer family, 1900

Saloon in Hillview

Albert McClay residence, Hillview, Illinois, 1909

Dining room, McClay Orchards

Train depot in Hillview, Illinois

The Phoenix Hotel, Hillview, Illinois 1915

Flood of Hillview, Illinois

Humbolt Patterson General Store

Hillview Jail, now used as a fire station, 2013

CHAPTER 26

October Harassment

Throughout these trying months, Charlie had continued with his duties as marshal, and at least one of the brothers was with him every day acting as his deputy. Some days it was a relief to walk the streets and try to clear his mind of the sadness that permeated the house after Everett Eugene's death. Other days he longed to be at home with Lucy even though neither seemed to be of much help to the other during the grieving process.

During the cold winter months, there was little trouble on the streets for which Charlie was thankful. The mayor often told Charlie he was glad to see that the streets were calm. Occasionally a minor argument broke out in one of the saloons. There had not been as much trouble at the railroad station so the jail had not had much use. Charlie and the mayor were beginning to believe that maybe these hoodlums were beginning to believe that Charlie was serious about making Hillview a safe place to live and visit. Even during the summer months, there had not been a lot of trouble. Charlie had heard that one of the main troublemakers, who he thought was the ringleader, had been gone for a while during those summer months. Maybe that was why there had been little trouble. However, just as all of them were enjoying a few peaceful days and nights, trouble reared its ugly head late in October.

It was a warm evening for October. There had been several enjoyable days everyone called Indian summer. Lucy,

Liz, and Ernest had gone to the prayer service on Wednesday night. As the three of them walked down the stone stairs, Ernest noticed several figures milling around across the street. As they moved in and out of the shadows, he recognized a couple of them as being part of the gang of ruffians that had caused trouble in the past months. His first thought was that the three of them should turn around, go back into the church, and wait to see if they would go away. He did not want to alarm Lucy and Liz, so he just hurried them along in the direction of the house. About halfway to the house, he looked over his shoulder and saw that they were being followed. Then the hollering and cursing started. He told Lucy and Liz to look straight ahead and walk as fast as they could. All of a sudden, one of the hoodlums ran up and tried to grab Liz. Ernest did not know how many there were, but knew he was outnumbered. At that moment, his main thought was that he had to protect Lucy and Liz, no matter what he had to do. His knew he needed to get them home safely as quickly as he could.

Just as that thought flew through his mind, he felt a glancing blow to the side of his head, which knocked him to his knees. Even though he was caught off guard, he was on his feet in a split second. He doubled up his fist and hit one of the hoodlums as hard as he could in the middle of his chest, knocking him to the ground. Ernest's days cutting wood had left him with a lean, hard, strong body. These hoodlums were a soft bunch and not nearly so brave when confronted by someone who fought back. They were used to pushing, shoving, and causing trouble with the townsfolk who tried to avoid them rather than stand up to them.

Lucy and Liz started screaming at the top of their lungs. In just a few seconds, Ernest realized that the hoodlums had taken off in the other direction. Those blood-curdling screams probably had people looking out their windows! Not taking any chances, Ernest grabbed both girls by their arms, and they scrambled over the railroad tracks toward the house as quickly as they could. As they rushed into the house, both girls were shaking and crying. Ernest was in a rage as he threw off his jacket.

"You cain't even go ta church in this damn town without gittin' harassed. Three 'r four o' those hoodlums who 're always hangin' around the street corners tried ta grab the girls an' were yellin' an' cussin'. They're probably some o' that gang that hangs 'round with Bum Deeds. It's a good thing I didn't have a gun with me, or I'd o' shot 'em."

Lucy was still shaking as Charlie put his arms around her. She leaned against his chest and said, "I hate this town. I want ta go back ta Mexico."

Jim, who had been quietly taking in the conversation, looked at Charlie and said, "These hoodlums are gittin' rough again. When they start pickin' on Lucy an' Liz, its time ta do more than just throw 'em in jail fer a night. I think we'd be smart if we armed ourselves. When they start attackin' us an' the girls, then it's time ta git real serious. A night in jail don't seem ta stop any o' the shit that goes on. I thought maybe things were goin' ta be okay, but I was wrong."

Charlie walked over to the window and stood staring out. His cheeks were becoming stained with red, and when this happened, you knew he was furious. He turned and quietly said, "Let me think 'bout that. Ernest, kin ya identify the ones who were bothering ya tonight? If ya kin, I'll have the circuit judge give me a warrant fer their arrest in the morning. We'll throw their asses in jail and charge 'em with assault. It'll be more'n an overnight stay then."

Jim shook his head and said, "Charlie, I ain't so sure. The judge'll jest fine 'em. Then somebody pays the fine, an' they're back on the street laughin' at us."

Dick, who had a short fuse, was irate at what had happened to Liz and Lucy. "I don't give a damn what happens. If I find those thugs, I'll carve 'em a new asshole."

Charlie looked sternly at his brothers and at Dick in particular, and said, "Let's hold on just a minute. First of all, I'm the marshal an' yer my deputies. Anythin' we do'll be inside the law. We cain't make a mistake an' do somethin' illegal they can pin on us. That's probably what they're hopin' fer so they'll have an excuse ta run us outta town. There's four of us, and if we tried ta round 'em all up at one time, there might be ten of 'em. Fer the most part, things have been kind o' quiet the past few weeks until this happened tonight. The idea of us carryin' guns ain't what I want ta do, but if ya feel things 're gittin' that dangerous, then I'll go along with it. I've been doin' pretty good with my cane, so I'll leave my gun at home. There's a reason this cane got the name of bein' a 'pain cane.'"

Earnest piped up and said, "Ya know, Charlie's right. If I would've had a gun tonight, I might o' killed somebody. Our job is ta keep the peace, not actin' like one o' them thugs we're tryin' ta control. Those thugs git full of liquor bought in Missouri an' come back on that five o'clock train and then start causin' trouble."

Jim shook his head and said, "Yer probably right, but it might be a good idea that when we're out after dark makin' sure the streets 're safe that two o' us go together from now on."

Charlie looked over at Dick and could tell that he was still fuming over what had happened.

"I agree with Ernest," Charlie said. "How 'bout you, Dick?"

"I can take care o' myself, but I'll go along with whatever ya say, Charlie."

Dick and Liz left the room as Dick was still mumbling to himself.

Chapter 27

An Unusual Offer

As usual, when Charlie had something serious to think over, he stayed up late that night chewing on a cigar, staring at the potbellied stove, and thinking about the incident that had taken place. As he sat staring, his eyes were drawn to the cabinet in the corner of the room, which held a gun that had been given to him by Albert McClay a few months earlier. He had wrapped it in brown paper and hidden it on the bottom shelf.

Albert McClay and the McClay family were a well-respected family in the Hillview community. They were the owners of the McClay Orchard, which was the largest employer in the area. They hired migrant workers on a seasonal basis, which could be as many as four hundred depending on the size of the apple crop. On occasion, these migrant workers would hang around with some of the thugs around the town and cause trouble in the streets. Mr. McClay could keep them working hard during the day, but he knew that during the evening hours, and particularly on the weekends, it was hard to keep them around the housing units. The local troublemakers knew that they could sell liquor to the migrant workers for more than what they paid for it in Missouri. Almost every day, one of two of the gang members hopped on the train to Missouri, brought liquor back, and sold it to the migrant workers. Mr. McClay had not found a way to control that situation.

Over the last few years, Mr. McClay had watched the crime increase in Hillview and did not like seeing what was happening to their little community. In recent years, those individuals who had been hired to enforce the law disappeared, or had been run out of town, which left the village with no law enforcement. As he watched Charlie and his brothers try to get a handle on the situation, he felt confident that if anyone could do it, they could. He knew Charlie did not carry a gun, though, and that he just used his cane when confronting those that were causing trouble. After giving the situation some thought, Mr. McClay decided to have a .32 Colt revolver specially made for Charlie. He felt strongly that Charlie should carry that gun with him and not rely on just his cane.

Early one day in the spring of 1914, Mr. McClay asked Mayor Coates to arrange a meeting with Charlie on a Saturday afternoon at the Phoenix Hotel. Charlie was surprised, as he had no idea what the meeting was to be about. When he walked in and saw the two men in the lobby, Charlie recalled that he was immediately on his guard, although he did not know exactly why. He knew Mayor Coates quite well and had met Mr. McClay on the street on several occasions but could not figure out why the two of them would want to meet with him.

After they shook hands and sat down at a table, Mr. McClay asked Charlie if there was anything he could do to help solve the gang problems. Charlie remembered being a little surprised by the question. After searching both men's faces for a few seconds, he decided he would just be very frank with them and said, "Just tell me who the ringleaders o' these gangs are an' who their parents 're or if they have any other relatives in town. I'll take care o' the rest. I got a pretty good idea but I'd like ta know what yer thoughts are. It seems like there're some townsfolk that don't like what's goin' on, but they don't want ta do anythin' if it involves somebody in their family."

Mr. McClay did not hesitate when he told Charlie that most people thought that Clarence "Bum" Deeds and Isom Leonard were the two ringleaders that the others seemed to follow. Deeds was a personable young man but seemed to have too much time on his hands, as did many of the young fellows. Too much time and too much liquor was a bad combination. When that occurred, they just started drinking early in the day, and then the trouble followed.

Charlie acknowledged that he was of the same opinion. About that time, Mr. McClay picked up a brown paper bag that had been in his lap. He set it on the table in front of Charlie and told him to open it. Charlie was perplexed and could not imagine what Mr. McClay would be giving him. He opened the paper bag and took out a brown leather case that was holding a 32-caliber Police Positive Colt revolver and a box of cartridges. Charlie looked at Mr. McClay and Mayor Coates with a questioning look. Mr. McClay told Charlie he had had the gun custom made for him because he thought Charlie might need it. He had heard snippets of conversations when he was around his migrant workers and just felt that Charlie needed to protect himself, particularly when he was on the streets at night.

Charlie was somewhat at a loss for words but assured Mr. McClay that all he needed was his cane. Mr. McClay did not appear to be convinced. He told Charlie to take the gun as a gift from him. Charlie knew firearms and knew that it was a very fine pistol. He was moved by Mr. McClay's concern and thanked him for his kind gesture. Charlie shook hands with Mr. McClay and the mayor and turned to leave. As he opened the door, he turned back to Mr. McClay and Mayor Coates and said, "Workin' fer folks like you makes this job worthwhile."

When Charlie arrived back at the house, he showed the gun to his brothers and told them where he had gotten it. Jim, who loved guns, fondled it as though it was the finest gun he had ever touched in his life. Jim looked at Charlie saying, "Maybe ya ought ta buy a holster and wear it on yer belt. Maybe it just might let them hoodlums know they'd better start toein' the line an' ya ain't messin' 'round anymore."

A sense of doom came over Charlie every time anyone started talking about having to use guns to quell the violence in the town. Today it seemed to be an even bigger weight on his chest, after his meeting with the mayor and Mr. McClay. He was a tenacious man, and he was confident that if his cane was good enough to get the job done on the railroad, then it ought to be good enough to clean up the streets of Hillview. He was still not convinced he needed to carry a gun, although he had to acknowledge that the trouble on the streets was beginning to escalate again. He had been able to take care of some of it for short periods of time but the trouble never seemed to go away totally. He would not be happy until the folks of town could walk the streets and be at the railroad station and not be afraid of the drunken gangs.

CHAPTER 28

Gunshots!

Not much out of the ordinary happened during the next few days, but Charlie and his brothers knew better than to be lulled into complacency. There were the usual skirmishes with some of the local ruffians, and a couple of them spent an occasional night in jail sleeping off a drunk, but there had been no trouble directed at Charlie or his family. Lucy and Liz's days took on a pattern of cooking, taking care of the house, and attending church. Jim, Ernest, and Dick spent time with Charlie filling their responsibility as deputies, and whenever they could, they went hunting and trapping. Occasionally they would all head to Mrs. Greene's Restaurant on Saturday night for supper. Lucy and Liz looked forward to those nights that Charlie asked them if they wanted to go, and, of course, he knew the answer even before he asked.

One night around midnight in the middle of December 1914, Jim woke up because the dogs were barking and raising quite a ruckus in their pen. He thought he heard the sound of gunshots but could not imagine why anyone would be shooting a gun at that time of night. He lit the kerosene lamp and walked to the back door. As he peered out the door, he could hear one of the dogs whining. About that time, another shot rang out. He heard the ping as the bullet hit very near the doorframe where he was standing. He quickly turned the kerosene light out and shut the door. He turned around to see Charlie coming down the hall. Even in the darkness of the room, Jim could see that Charlie's face lined with worry. "What the hell's goin' on?" asked Charlie. "I thought I heard gunshots."

Jim was peering out the window trying to see what was going on. He whispered, "Ya did hear some shots. Somebody took a shot at me when I opened the door. It sounded like it came from up there on the hill near the woods. I think somebody shot at my dogs. I can hear one of 'em whinin'."

There was a full moon illuminating the backyard, and Jim could see the dog pen. It looked like two of the dogs were lying down, and one was still whining. These dogs weren't just dogs; they were Jim's buddies. With anger flashing across his face, he turned to Charlie, "I gotta go outside an' check on my dogs. One of 'em's hurt."

Charlie put his hand on Jim's shoulder and said, "If ya go out there right now, you'll be an easy target as bright as that moon is. They already took one shot at ya. They might not miss next time."

Jim pondered the situation for a few moments. "Okay, but I'm goin' ta watch, an' soon as I see some clouds goin' over the moon, I'm goin' out there. I'll bet it's those thugs from town, an' I don't think they're goin' ta hang around in the woods all night. Now that they know we're up, they've probably hightailed it outta there."

Jim hurried to his room to jerk on a pair of pants and grab a coat. Charlie stood watch at the window to see if he could see any movement but saw nothing. Jim came back and stood by Charlie as they watched for a dark cloud to move across the moon, blocking the light that it was throwing off. As soon as Jim thought he could make it, he tore off through the yard to the dog pen. He crouched down by the dogs lying on the ground and was heartsick. He could see that two of them were dead and the third one, Old One Eye, had a flesh wound. He picked him up in his arms and ran as fast as he could run into the house.

Fortunately, a bullet had only grazed Old One Eye's leg, but Jim needed to clean the wound and stop the bleeding. Jim sat on the cold floor in front of the potbellied stove with the dog in his lap trying to keep him warm. Tears streamed down his face over the loss of his other two dogs.

No one had ever seen Jim shed tears. Jim made a bed by the potbellied stove for Old One Eye and brought food and water to him. No one dared suggest that Old One Eye did not belong in the front room. They knew what those dogs meant to Jim. The next day, Dick worked alongside of Jim as they spent the morning digging a grave in the frozen ground for the two dogs that had been shot to death. The ground was frozen and hard, but Jim was determined to get the job done. When the dogs had been buried, Dick was just about as frozen as the ground and went inside to get warm. Jim squatted by the gravesite for quite some time grieving for his buddies. The whole household felt his sadness because they knew how much he loved those dogs.

When Jim came stomping back into the house, they could see the anger in his eyes as he said, "If I find the son of a bitch that killed my dogs, he's a dead man!" He headed out the door, and they knew he was headed to town to see if he could hear anything that might give him a clue as to who the culprits were. They knew that the thugs quite often started drinking early in the day, and by evening, started bragging about some of the pranks they had pulled and the trouble they had started. If anyone was out there talking, Jim was going to find out.

Charlie was aware that Jim had a 22 pistol he carried when he checked his trap lines, but he did not want Jim using it on someone if he found out who killed his dogs. Charlie thought back to an incident that had happened a week or so earlier and wondered if it had anything to do with the shooting of the dogs. Jim had taken one of the hoodlums from a neighboring town to jail one night and had been a little rough with him. When Charlie stopped by Mrs. Greene's for a cup of coffee one afternoon, he heard that the fellow was going to be gunning for Jim.

Charlie never thought too much more about it, since the hoodlums that hung around were always spouting off about what they were going to do. Drinking seemed to be their pastime. When they had too much, they started feeling brave and tossed threats around. So far, none of their threats had materialized, although Charlie tried to stay on the lookout whenever he heard something. With what had happened last night to Jim's dogs, Charlie realized that he was going to have to listen to the talk more carefully and take it more seriously. Knowing what mood Jim was in, Charlie decided it was best to keep quiet for the time being.

The next day Charlie made it a point to tell Mayor Coates of the incident. "I'm not takin' any more o' this bullshit regardless o' who is responsible. I've tried ta clean this town up, but if anybody thinks they can git away with shootin' Jim's dogs and takin' a shot at my house, they're dead wrong! When it gits personal with my family, somethin' has ta change. The village council seems ta want us ta do it usin' kid gloves, but that don't seem ta work. We've tried it that way now fer over a year. Now, we're goin' ta do it my way."

It was a hard thing to admit, but Charlie was beginning to come to the realization that the undercurrent of animosity toward him and his brothers was escalating. He had to figure out a way to stop it before one of his family members was seriously hurt or killed.

CHAPTER 29

Christmas Eve, 1914

Charlie did not know if the younger ones in other families were always the ones that could find trouble, but he knew it was that way in their family. Harry was a good kid, but Dick was a magnet for trouble. As Dick was growing up, if there was some kind of trouble around town, he seemed to be in the middle of it. Charlie knew that Dick liked to hit the bottle, and when he did, he became aggressive and mouthy. Before Dick had married Liz and brought her to Hillview, Charlie had thrown him in a jail cell for an overnight stay a time or two just to sober him up. Once he and Liz were married, Liz was able to put a reign on Dick, and he did not spend as much time in the saloons. He had hoped that Liz would always be able to keep the strings tight, but their marital bliss did not last very long.

On Christmas Eve, Dick and Liz had a rather heated argument everyone in the house could hear. With angry words flying in all directions, Dick stomped out of the bedroom, jerked on his coat and best felt hat, and stormed out the door. Everyone knew he was heading to one of the saloons. Where else would he go at this time of night on Christmas Eve? It was cold and windy outside, and smoke curled out of the chimneys in a sideways motion. Dick was so mad, he did not care how cold it was.

When Dick entered the saloon, there were only a couple of people standing at the bar, and they soon shuffled out the door. The tables stood empty in the corners of the room. It was Christmas Eve, and most people were at home or at a church service with their families As Dick rushed through the door, he stood for a moment to let his eyes adjust to the dimness. He threw his coat and hat on the pegs by the door, walked up to the bar, and hollered for a drink. The bartender looked up in dismay and let out a groan. The last thing he wanted to do was to have to pour drinks all evening for a fellow that looked like he had just eaten a bear. He was well acquainted with Dick and knew that Dick liked to drink. After several drinks, the bartender told Dick he wanted to close up early since it was Christmas Eve.

The place was empty and the streets were quiet. The bartender told Dick he wanted to go home to his family and that Dick should just get on home too. By then, Dick had had enough to drink that he was beginning to feel sorry for himself. He whined to the bartender, "It's Christmas Eve an' Liz kicked me outta the house, so let's jus' have one more drink." The bartender knew that one more drink was not what Dick needed.

About that time, they felt a cold rush of air as the saloon door opened. A fairly well dressed man of about thirty-five, who the bartender had seen around town a few times, staggered through the door. He looked around the saloon and then looked straight at Dick. After a moment's pause, he grabbed Dick's hat off of the peg, threw it on the floor, put his foot on top of it, ground it into the floor, and said, "You son of a bitch! You been foolin' around with my wife, and I'm goin' to grind you into the floor just like I did your hat."

Dick had a short temper even when he was not drinking. When he was drinking, that fuse was even shorter. He turned around and leaned back against the bar.

"Even if I was foolin' 'round with yer wife, that's no reason ta ruin my good hat."

As he was saying this, Dick reached down into his boot, pulled out a straight razor and started toward the man. When the man saw the straight razor and the look in Dick's eyes, he turned and staggered back out of the door shouting over his shoulder, "You Witwer brothers ought to be run out of town."

Dick put his razor back in his boot, turned to the bartender, and chuckled. "If he'd take care o' his wife, somebody else wouldn't have ta."

The bartender finally convinced Dick that he had to leave because he was going to close up. Dick walked unsteadily to where his hat was on the floor, picked it up, and jerked his coat off the peg. Before he could make it to the door, the bartender rushed over to open it. He practically shoved Dick out the door so he could quickly lock it.

On Christmas morning, Dick woke up with what he thought was the worst hangover he had ever had. He tried to roll over in bed, and it felt like a thousand knives stabbing through his rib cage. He sure was not going to try that again. He tried to push himself up in bed, and his wrist gave way under the weight of his body. Lightening pains went through his hand and up his arm. His head was throbbing, his lips felt swollen, and he could feel a gash on his head. After focusing for a couple of minutes, he felt Liz's stare as she sat in a straight-back chair by the door with a grim look on her face.

Through a few loose front teeth he said, "I feel terrible. What the hell happened ta me?"

Before Liz could answer, Ernest and Jim walked into the room with disgusted looks on their faces. Ernest was the first one to speak. "Ya look like you've been worked over with a baseball bat. It's a good thing Liz started ta worry 'bout ya last night. When ya didn't come home, she asked us ta go see if we could find ya. You'd o' been froze ta death in that alley if we hadn't found ya.

Nothin' was open so we started lookin' in the streets an' alleys tryin' ta find ya. We finally found ya behind the saloon all beat up, an' we had ta carry ya home. All ya did was mumble somethin' 'bout yer hat. We tried ta find Doc Garrison but he's outta town over Christmas."

Dick mumbled, "I feel awful."

At that moment, no one felt much pity for Dick and the way he felt. Liz was so mad she could not even bring herself to say anything. Jim just glared at him and said, "Dammit, you're twenty-two years old. Ain't ya ever goin' ta learn ta stay out a trouble? Ya sure know how ta screw up a holiday. Lucy and Liz have been cookin' us a Christmas dinner fer two days. Mom, Dad, and Harry surprised us last night. They come all the way over from Mexico so we're all together fer Christmas, an' you pull a stunt like this. Are ya goin' ta lay there in that bed all day or are ya goin' ta git up?"

With his head pounding, his ribs on fire, his wrist the size of a grapefruit, and blood caked on his head, Dick looked miserably at his wife and his two brothers. As all three of them continued staring at him, waiting for an explanation, he struggled to sit up in bed. He was in no shape to even swing his legs over the side of the bed much less get out of bed! As he fell back onto the pillow, he started to remember a little of what had taken place before he left the saloon.

Through the fog in his brain, Dick remembered the fellow that had come into the bar, stomped on his hat, and accused him of messing around with his wife. He sure was not going to mention that in front of Liz and did not want his brothers to know about it either. He ignored the question Jim had asked him and bellowed, "Those bastards ruined my hat. They must've jumped me when I left the saloon. I don't want anythin' ta eat but I sure could use a drink."

"You ain't gittin' no drink. You must've had too much ta drink last night ta git yourself in such a mess," replied Ernest. "Liz, maybe ya can git a pan of warm water and git him cleaned up a little, not that he deserves bein' helped."

Dick stayed in bed all day while the rest of the family celebrated the holiday, although everyone was a little more subdued than usual. They did not feel any pity for Dick but knew that it was a difficult day, particularly for Liz and Nancy. Dick's escapade had put a damper on the day for everyone. Later in the evening, Charlie walked into the bedroom and asked Liz to leave the room. She had gone in to see if Dick wanted anything to eat. Charlie, with his eyes narrowed and ablaze in anger, said, "This is the last time I'm goin' ta tell ya. Either straighten up 'r go back ta Missouri. This bullshit o' yours could git ya killed 'r cause harm ta come ta one of us 'r cause all of us ta lose our jobs. I ain't riskin' my job just cause ya cain't stay outta the bottle."

Dick looked rather contrite and did not say a word. He just nodded as Charlie turned and walked out of the room, but he made a promise to himself that no one would ever get the best of him again. It was a good thing Charlie could not hear his thoughts.

CHAPTER 30

The Calm before the Storm

It was a few days before Dick was able to get out of bed and run the traps again with Jim. Nobody was going to let him lie around in bed any longer than absolutely necessary. The first day he had to get up at four o'clock on a cold morning to run those traps reminded him of every ache and pain. Jim was relentless in making him do his end of the work. That winter the two of them had set over fifty traps. They trapped a lot of wild mink and other fur-bearing animals. The price of prime pelts was at an all-time high, and both men liked the extra money they made, some of which they contributed to the household expenses. Running a trap line and being deputies kept both of them busy. Charlie went with them occasionally, but since coming to Hillview, Charlie left most of the hunting and trapping to the other three.

There was a lot of competition to find good hunting and trapping locations. Occasionally, the men who trapped talked about their traps being stolen. After a while, though, it became apparent that this was happening more frequently with Jim and Dick's traps. They finally approached Charlie to talk about it. Jim told Charlie he had been hanging around Mrs. Greene's Restaurant when he had some free time just to see if he could hear any gossip about whether or not anybody else was losing traps. He had asked some of the other fellows but nobody else seemed to be having much trouble. The three of them began to wonder if they were being targeted and it was just their traps that were being stolen. There had been some scuttlebutt about the Witwer brothers encroaching on the territory for trapping, most of which came from the fellows who hung around the street corners. No one thought much about this because they did not like anything about the Witwer brothers and did not hesitate to criticize everything they did. They were very outspoken about their feelings. Some of those fellows had no full-time employment, and trapping was one way they made their money, most of which was probably spent on liquor.

Killing rabbits and ducks and selling this wild game, to be shipped down the river to St. Louis on a pack boat, was a way to make good money. The Witwer brothers were as good at it as anyone was. As time passed, it was obvious that more resentment was building toward the Witwer brothers for being involved in hunting and trapping. First, Jim's dogs had been killed, and now the traps were being stolen. There was too much going on for it all to be coincidence.

The hoodlums and gangs had not been roaming the streets or hanging around the railroad station causing as much trouble during those cold winter days, but Charlie felt an underlying current of hostility everywhere he went. Sometimes there were arguments in the saloons, usually on the weekend that escalated to street fights. Charlie would have to use his cane to break the fight up and send everybody on their way. He could handle these situations. He just wanted the streets to be safe for the townsfolk.

Charlie put forth a lot of effort to make the rounds of the businesses every few days just to keep in touch with the business owners and to see what the townsfolk had to say when he encountered them on the street. He oftentimes felt uneasiness as he talked to various people and was not sure what the problem was. He knew that throughout the sixteen months he had been the marshal, several of those who ended up in his jail were sons, relatives or family friends of some of the so-called pillars of the community. He did not know if this was the root of the uneasiness and animosity or not. He had been hired to make sure the troublemakers in the area did not take over the streets, and that was just what he was doing, no matter whose toes he stepped on. He had warned them when he took the job that he would get the job done, one way or another.

Charlie was not a quitter. He was determined to make the streets of Hillview safe, but there were times when he wondered if it would just be better for everyone if he tried to get his job back as a detective on the railroad. Quite often, Lucy and Liz were upset, and he knew they worried about him and his brothers, particularly when they went out at night. And, he worried about the safety of his family.

As the winter days and weeks rolled by, no matter what Charlie did, he was unable to shake the nagging feeling he had. The gangs seemed to become even more resentful of Charlie and his brothers and were very vocal about it. What bothered Charlie most was that not all of their aggression was directed only at Charlie and his brothers. There were rumors floating around that some of the hoodlums intended to eliminate not only the village marshal and his deputies but the mayor as well. And it was not by voting them out! From the gossip he overheard, their means of eliminating them was far more sinister than casting a vote! Charlie knew these hoodlums had no respect for the law, and rumor was that they intended to do something about it. There had been various rumors floating around before but none that were this serious.

This rumor of "eliminating certain people" had been floating around since the Fourth of July picnic the summer before. Charlie had not taken it too seriously at that time, but the tension had been escalating over the months. He and all of his brothers had been on duty on the Fourth because he did not want any trouble during the daylong celebration. A couple of days later, one of the businessmen told Charlie that one of the thugs had been overheard saying, "If the mayor and the village marshal and his brothers don't leave town, we'll bury 'em." At that time, no one ever came forth with just exactly who had made that statement, but the rumor seemed to stay afloat all winter rather than dying out.

By this time, Charlie knew every one of those thugs, knew who their parents were, who they were related to in the community, and how each family was tied to other families through close friendships. That information did not make Charlie's job any easier.

As the months passed, Charlie felt like people were choosing sides, and there was a widening division between whose side everyone was on. Some of the folks in the community thought Charlie and his brothers were making every effort to clean up the violence in the streets; others thought they were not. Then, others wanted the violence cleaned up as long as it did not affect anyone in their family or their friends' families. That seemed to be where the biggest hang-up was. Occasionally, Charlie was plagued by doubts of which side of the law everyone was on. Sometimes his enthusiasm for his job waned. He knew it was a volatile situation that was growing worse as the days went by.

The justice of the peace set up a courtroom just about any place he wanted to. Sometimes he used one of the rooms at the hotel or the jail, and on occasion, he set up court in one of the saloons. Charlie was not in agreement with handling things in this manner but it only caused more dissension if he expressed his opinion. Most of the charges against those who were arrested were for public drunkenness, disorderly conduct, or some other misdemeanor charge. A fine would be levied, or sometimes the offender would be sentenced to another day or two in jail. The justice never gave much credence to the fact that these same individuals came before him repeatedly. When a fine was levied, someone in the family simply paid the fine. Nothing did much to curtail trouble. The coffers of the town were much fuller than before Charlie came to Hillview, but that was the only positive result.

Charlie got to the point where he rarely worked a day by himself, always having one of his brothers acting as deputy. This way, he had a backup in case there was a lot of trouble, but the main reason for doing this was he always wanted to have a witness in the event of an arrest. He knew the only way he could get anything done in front of the justice of the peace was to have a witness. Sometimes Charlie thought that even having a witness had little impact on the outcome. He was beginning to wonder if the justice of the peace was making a little extra money on the side by being so lenient.

There were many times when Charlie doubted whether having his brothers as deputies had been the best decision. Some of the thugs claimed that the deputy would say anything that Charlie told him to say, even if it was not the truth. By the first of the year, Charlie had been in Hillview for over a year, and he had to admit that there had been little progress made in making Hillview a safer place to live. Too many threads were beginning to unravel, and Charlie strongly sensed the underlying current of turmoil.

There were so many rumors by the first of the year that Charlie dreaded going to the post office or to Mrs. Greene's Restaurant, but he knew that he had to stay in contact with the townsfolk. One day when Charlie was sitting on a stool in Mrs. Greene's Restaurant having a piece of pie, he overheard a conversation that possibly not all of the fines being collected were being turned over to the town council. Charlie was not sure if they were talking loud enough for him to hear on purpose, or if they just did not realize he was sitting at the counter. Charlie might be accused of doing some things wrong, but one thing for sure was that he was an honest man. No money ever found its way to his or his brothers' pockets.

Most of the time, it was Charlie's responsibility to collect the fines. If he could not do it personally, he always sent two deputies. He cautioned them to never use any methods that were not within the law, but he had heard there were complaints.

Another rumor that had been circulating around the community was that the village council was considering a special vote of the residents of Hillview to determine whether to keep Charlie as their village marshal. Because Mayor Coates had been instrumental in encouraging the council to appoint Charlie, some of the animosity toward Charlie and his brothers bled over to Mayor Coates.

Once a rumor gets started, particularly in a small community, it takes on a life of its own. Mrs. Greene's Restaurant was abuzz most mornings. Of course, no one ever knew who started the rumor, or if there was any truth to it, or where he had heard it first, but after being told a few times, it was told for the truth—and probably bigger than when it started. There was always someone willing to let Charlie or one of the brothers know what he or she had heard.

The one rumor that aggravated Charlie the most was when Lucy and Liz came home and told him that some of the women were saying they heard that Charlie had threatened Mr. Mundy, the president of the village council, along with some of the other council members, if they tried to get rid of him as the village marshal. Charlie was furious but knew that trying to defend himself would not do a bit of good. It would probably only make matters worse. He had not had any direct confrontations with Mr. Mundy or any of the council members. He had attended a few of the meetings throughout the months to try to get more support. Sometimes when he left the meeting, he was not very happy, but he had never threatened anyone.

With all this turmoil going on, Charlie felt that some of the residents, which included a council member or two, thought that he and his brothers were just about as bad as the gangs they were hired to control. Whether that was justified or not was a matter of opinion, and it certainly was not Charlie's opinion.

One Sunday evening, as Charlie and his brothers sat around drinking coffee and hashing out all that had taken place since they had moved to Hillview, Charlie thought back to a few weeks earlier when he had been called before the village council meeting. The council had expressed their concern about his actions and those of his brothers in their dealings with individuals they put in jail. Charlie had not discussed what had happened at the meeting with his brothers, but as they talked that evening, he told them what the council members had said to him and how he had responded.

"I know I cain't remember zactly what I said, but it was somethin' like, 'since I've been village marshal, the streets 're some safer. Yer wives an' daughters ain't bein' heckled as much by drunks. There ain't been nobody murdered since Slick, the gambler, was thrown under the train. There ain't been no mysterious disappearances. We ain't found nobody mysteriously drowned in their own well. It seems as though a lot o' what has taken place has been directed at me an' my family. My house has been shot at. My brother's dogs was killed. Dick was nearly beat to a pulp on Christmas Eve. There's rumors floating 'round 'bout death threats, but that don't slow me down none. Ya know it was worse 'round here before ya hired me. An' if ya want to fire me, those hoodlums that hang 'round the train station will o' won. Ya cain't have it both ways. Either I do it my way or ya can have my badge.' I ain't heard no more from 'em one way or ta other."

Charlie was not a man to lose control of his temper often, but he remembered being so angry his head throbbed from the blood racing through so fast. He knew those council members were not happy with his attitude or his response, but he meant every word he said. It made him just about as mad thinking back on it.

With their chairs pushed back and legs stretched out toward the potbellied stove, the Witwer brothers' conversation came to a sobering silence. Charlie discussed very little at home, mostly because he did not want to cause Lucy and Liz to be upset. He was sure they heard enough when they went to town and to church, and they did not need to hear more around the house.

As he sat there, he thought about another incident that probably caused a rift between himself and some of the church-going residents in Hillview. One of the pastors of a local church asked the village council if they would have Charlie investigate to see if there was prostitution going on. It seemed as though several church members from three of the local churches had been talking to each other about the subject and was sure that there was some prostitution activity right under their noses. Finding prostitutes was not high on Charlie's agenda, and he told the council as much. He was sure this did not win him any support from the church community.

Charlie knew Lucy and Liz would be more than happy if he and Dick told them they were quitting and moving back to Mexico. Charlie knew Jim would follow them wherever they went. He was not sure what was going on with Ernest. He was spending his days off with their brother, Frank. Quitting was just not a word in Charlie's vocabulary, though, so he did not give this idea much more than a fleeting thought.

The four of them sat staring at nothing in particular and knew there would not be any solutions found that night.

CHAPTER 31

The Challenge: March 5, 1915

Early in March, Dick was at the McClay residence repairing Mrs. McClay's sewing machine. He had not forgotten the skill he had learned in the Booneville Correction Center, and every once in a while, one of the women would ask him to fix her machine. It was just about dusk when he left the McClay residence, and instead of walking home the way he usually did, the lure of having a drink got the best of him. He had not gotten into much trouble since Christmas Eve, and the lights in the saloon seemed to be beckoning him. He thought he would just drop in for a quick drink and then be on his way home. He knew Liz would be waiting for him, and he sure did not want to get into any trouble and have Charlie mad at him.

As Dick stepped into the saloon and looked around, he noticed there were a couple of tables in the back where several of the local residents were playing poker. There was a city ordinance against gambling, so they played with poker chips on the table, but everyone knew they settled later for the cash that the bartender was holding. Charlie had more important things to take care of, so this was one city ordinance that was not enforced.

Being a deputy, playing poker with these fellows was not something Dick should have involved himself in, but Dick did not always use the best judgment. After he ordered a drink at the bar, Dick picked up his glass in one hand and ambled back to the poker tables swinging his sewing machine toolbox in his other hand.

"Got any room fer another player?"

One of the players answered, "I'd just as soon take money from a deputy as to take it from anybody else."

Dick went up to the bar and handed the bartender a few bills in return for some chips. Not only had he picked up the skill of fixing sewing machines at the correctional center, but he had also pick up some good math skills. One of Dick's other brothers, Frank, had taught him the game of poker when he was barely into his teens.

Dick just grinned at the card players sitting around the table and pulled up a chair with an air of confidence. After a few hours of playing, the bartender came back to the table and told them it was time to shut the game down and cash in their chips. Everyone cashed in their chips and headed out the door. Dick did not seem to be in any hurry. By the time he cashed in his chips, there was no one left in the bar except for the bartender. By this time, Dick had had several drinks and was feeling good, particularly since he had been winning all evening. He picked up his sewing machine repair box and headed for the door.

Dick had been so engrossed in the poker game that he had paid little attention to a few of the local ruffians drinking at the bar while the game was going on. As he grabbed his hat and coat and walked out the door, he noticed Isom Leonard leaning against the post in front of the saloon. When Dick glanced around, he saw a few other fellows milling around in the street, and they did not look too friendly. Dick knew that Charlie and Isom had had words on more than one occasion, and Charlie had threatened to throw the book at him. Charlie told him he would be spending more than just a night in the jail if he had to arrest him again.

It was late and the streets were deserted. Dick realized he was outnumbered, but his first instinct was to pull out the straight razor that was in his boot. He had lost one on Christmas Eve, but it had not taken him long to get another one. Even though he had had several drinks, he was clearheaded enough to remember Charlie's threat on Christmas Day, so he just stood in front of the door staring at Isom. He did not want to get on Charlie's bad side and be sent back to Mexico.

Unsteady on his feet, Isom held onto the post in front of the saloon and growled, "I want you to take a message to that brother of yours. Tell him he ain't man enough to take me in."

As those in the street edged closer to Dick, he started to squat to set his sewing machine repair box down and pull the straight razor out of his boot. Just about that time, he heard the squeak of the door and footsteps behind him. The bartender was standing in the doorway with his Billy club in hand. At the sight of the bartender and the Billy club, Isom and his buddies looked at one another and started backing away. They turned and quickly headed down the street. Dick turned around with a lopsided grin on his face. With his confidence boosted by all he had had to drink, he said, "I 'preciate yer help, but I could o' handled those thugs."

The bartender just nodded with a knowing look on his face as he turned around and walked back into the bar. Dick glanced back again as he heard the lock on the door click. As he stood on the steps of the saloon, he took a deep breath to clear his head. It was a dark night, and the clouds would occasionally break apart to let the moon shine through. The streets were empty, and he knew he needed to get home as quickly as he could. Not only would Liz be mad, but he did not want to have any more encounters with Isom and his gang. He kept looking over his shoulder as he made his way across the railroad tracks and up to the house. He hoped to be able to slip into the house without waking anyone, particularly Liz, but he knew that was probably not likely. He planned to tell Charlie the next morning what Isom had said, but he did not want to face him tonight either.

Dick woke up early the next morning but did not dare stay in bed even though his head was pounding and the light hurt his eyes. He would like to have turned over and pulled the covers over his head but knew that he could not get away with it. As he walked into the kitchen for a cup of coffee, Charlie looked up at him.

"I heard ya come in last night. You must've been at the saloon playing cards an' drinkin' too much. Did ya win or lose?"

Dick, trying to avoid Liz's angry look, poured himself a cup of coffee with an unsteady hand and said, "I think I won more'n what I lost. But, we got a problem with Isom Leonard an' his gang. He said ta tell ya that there was no way ya were ever goin' ta take 'im in."

Charlie gave Dick a long look. "We'll see 'bout that. If I see 'im drunk an' bein' disorderly one more time, he's goin' ta be spendin' more'n a night or two in jail. That's what I tol' 'im"

In his haste to get out of the kitchen and avoid a lecture from Liz about staying out late and drinking, Dick hit the corner of the table and coffee splashed out of his cup. Lucy picked up the dishrag to clean up the mess and told him to get out of the house. He had not had any breakfast, and his stomach was growling. After taking a quick look at Liz, Lucy and Charlie, he decided he should head for the door and forget about breakfast.

Charlie sat staring out the window and continued drinking his coffee. He seemed to spend a lot of time trying to figure things out, and he was not making much headway. As Charlie started to get his coat on and head to the jail, Ernest came into the kitchen and said he wanted to talk to him. Ernest told Charlie that he was not going to be staying in Hillview much longer. He wanted to move to New

Berlin, Illinois, to do farm work. Farming was his dream, and he thought it was time to make the move. He had made a few trips to Springfield to see his brother Frank when Charlie let him have a day or two off. Frank had introduced him to the Milby family, who owned a farm in the New Berlin area, which was about fifteen miles west of Springfield. He loved being around people who talked farming. Charlie knew this about Ernest, but he was still surprised.

Ernest said he had become acquainted with a pretty, red-haired daughter in the Milby family named Bertha. Ernest did not talk much about things but had quietly gotten a divorce from Sadie a few months earlier. He was a free man, and Bertha had certainly caught his eye. He told Charlie he just might ask Bertha to marry him when he got to New Berlin if things worked out. He was planning to work on the Milby farm.

When Ernest told Charlie of his decision, Charlie, being a man of few words, just shook his head, giving Ernest his usual reply when he thought a mistake was about to be made: "Ain't ya never goin' ta learn?" Charlie made this same comment to each of his brothers on occasions when he felt they were making unwise decisions. Charlie understood Ernest's decision to work on a farm but was most concerned that Ernest would make a hasty decision to get married again.

As Charlie sat back down at the table, he did not have any clear solution on how to solve the problems in Hillview. He knew the only thing he could tell Jim and Dick was that they would just have to keep on doing what they had been doing—try to keep the streets of Hillview safe for the honest, hard-working, family-oriented people of the community who just want to have a peaceful existence and raise their families. Charlie knew he would be one deputy short when Ernest left, but he would deal with that too. He walked out into the yard where Jim and Dick were standing and told them to go on about their business for the day, and he would see them at suppertime. Jim and Dick were a little baffled at Charlie's attitude, but both of them headed downtown.

CHAPTER 32

A Bad Omen: March 6, 1915

On Saturday, March 6, Charlie and the three brothers were sitting around the kitchen table as usual, coffee cup in hand. Charlie and Jim had come in from being downtown. Ernest and Dick had been working in the garden most of the morning trying to get it ready for planting potatoes. Lucy and Liz had fixed a large kettle of ham and beans. Lucy had to stretch their meat, so there were a lot more beans than ham. Jacob and Nancy had moved to Hillview just a few days earlier, so now there were two more to feed. Harry was staying with a family in Mexico. Everyone welcomed Jacob and Nancy into the household even though the house was small, and they were rather crowded. Lucy knew how to fix a pan full of delicious, sweet cornbread, which was the perfect addition to the pot of beans. The smell of it was dancing through the air. As soon as everyone walked into the house, they could smell what they were having for dinner.

After dinner, the four brothers sat back from the table with their legs stretched out. Everyone had gotten their fill so they all had contented looks on their faces. That did not last long, though, as the conversation turned to Isom Leonard and his buddies.

Lucy and Liz were cleaning up the table, anxious to leave the kitchen. Jacob and Nancy had gone to the front room to sit around the stove. Since they had moved to Hillview, Jacob spent most afternoons reading while Nancy sat knitting or doing needlework. Charlie and his brothers sat at the table as Lucy and Liz worked around them. They were hashing over what Dick had told them about his confrontation with Isom Leonard the night before as he left the saloon. The gangs were still making life difficult for residents and any visitors who passed through, particularly at the train station.

Charlie said, "Every time I arrest one o' those bastards fer gittin' into a fight, the one they beat up is afraid ta testify against 'em."

Dick, who was always the hothead, piped up and said, "Instead of arrestin' the bastards an' throwin' 'em in jail, let's just take 'em down ta the river an' throw their asses in. If the current is strong enough, we won't have ta worry 'bout 'em no more."

Ernest, who was far more reasonable, scoffed. "That kind o' harebrained idea will git us behind bars instead o' them. You might not mind sleepin' off a drunk in one o' them cells, but I don't want ta be spendin' any time in one."

Charlie commented, "Jus' be patient. They ain't licked us yet. I talked ta Sheriff Jessie Edwards here in Greene County, an' he said he'd back us up all the way."

As usual, Mrs. Greene's Restaurant and Patterson's Store were the places to learn what was going on around town. Sometimes people talked openly when Charlie or the other three were around, and sometimes they seemed to clam up. The last thing Charlie had heard was that a couple of the thugs around town had threatened a member of the village council and some of the townsfolk if they sided with the Witwer brothers. They seemed to be getting more brazen with their threats.

Charlie and his three brothers had taken a rather rough approach in recent weeks in dealing with the troublemakers when they took them into the jailhouse. This seemed to scare some of them, but there were a few for whom it did not matter what happened. Nothing seemed to be effective as Charlie tried to stop them from drinking and causing trouble.

Charlie had discussed with Sheriff Edwards the threats that were supposed to have been against some of the village residents, but they both knew there was not much that could be done as long as nothing came of the threats. Charlie was sure the threats had been made, and it was not just idle gossip, because several of the residents made every effort to avoid him. He could understand if their lives had been threatened if they sided with him. He knew that some of the other residents felt that he and his brothers were getting to be too harsh in dealing with the troublemakers, but nothing else had been working. Charlie had concluded that it was time to fight fire with fire, though.

Even though Charlie still had the 32-caliber pistol given to him by Albert McClay, he rarely carried it. Instead, Charlie preferred using his cane—his "pain cane"—when arresting someone or when he had to get a troublesome situation under control. This pain cane was a steel rod rapped in leather and about thirty-seven inches long. It was heavy enough to have about the same impact as a baseball bat.

Late in the afternoon, Charlie remembered he had not checked the post office box for his mail in a couple of days. He found Lucy and his mother, Nancy, in the kitchen beginning to prepare supper.

"Lucy, I'm goin' ta go down ta the post office before it closes an' pick up the mail. I shouldn't be gone more'n an hour."

Nancy looked up with a serious look on her lined face, walked over to Charlie, and put her hand on his arm, "Charlie, I don't think ya should go ta the post office today."

Charlie looked down at his mother. "I suppose ya got one of yer bad feelin's again."

Nancy gave him a long, sober look with concern in her eyes and shook her head. "I think ya should stay home. Supper's goin' ta be ready in a little while. We're havin' chicken an' dumplin's, one o' yer favorites.

Charlie just grinned at her, grabbed his hat, and headed for the door. He turned around and said, "I'll make it quick. How 'bout thirty minutes? Since yer cookin' my favorite, I sure don't want ta miss this supper."

Charlie picked up his cane that was sitting by the front door and headed out the door. He hesitated on the porch for a couple of minutes and abruptly turned around. Lucy and Nancy heard him come back in and heard his footsteps in the front room. Lucy walked out of the kitchen in time to see him go to the cabinet where he had stored the 32 caliber pistol Mr. McClay had given to him. She watched Charlie unwrap it from the brown paper, load it, and slip it into his hip pocket. She was perplexed, as she knew he rarely took it out of the cabinet.

As Charlie put the gun in his pocket, he told himself that he was not expecting any trouble, but his mother's words were rolling around in his thoughts. Charlie looked up and saw Lucy watching him. He walked over, gave her a quick hug, and bolted out of the front door. He did not want to get into a discussion with Lucy about the gun.

Charlie headed up the street, across the railroad tracks and across Hurricane Creek Bridge toward the main part of town carrying his cane. He figured he could get to the post office and back home in about twenty-five minutes if he hurried and did not stop to talk to anybody. It was about 4:45 p.m., so he would be back at the house eating those dumplings in a short while. Just the thought of them made his mouth water. It was Saturday, and he had spent most of the day reflecting back over the events of the past months, thinking about all of the setbacks that had occurred. He was not one to talk to anyone else much but kept most of it inside. Tonight he was ready to just have a good supper and relax.

CHAPTER 33

Kill or Be Killed: March 6, 1915

Clarence Deeds got up earlier than usual on that same Saturday. He had planned to go fishing with several of his buddies that morning. As he left the Deeds family home where he lived with his mother, aunt, and his grandfather, Clarence said, "I'll be back around noon with a mess of fish and I'll cook 'em up for supper." His mom was surprised to hear him say this. It was a rare occasion that Clarence stayed home in the evening, particularly on a Saturday night. She knew he usually met up with Isom Leonard and knew that sometimes, that meant trouble. She thought Isom was the instigator in making trips to Louisiana, Missouri, for the purpose of buying alcohol. Everybody in Hillview called it "fightin' whiskey" because somebody usually ended up in a fight. She did not like Clarence hanging around with the local fellows that drank too much and roamed the streets, but she did not have much influence over him.

About two o'clock in the afternoon, Clarence came in with about a dozen blue catfish. He spent the afternoon cleaning them. Once that was done, he cleaned up and told his mom he was going to the railroad station for a little while to meet Isom. His grandfather, who was sitting in a rocking chair in the front room, looked over his spectacles at Clarence and said, "Isom is going to be the death of you. You ought to stay away from him."

"We're just goin' to hang around downtown for a while, and then I'll be home and we'll eat some catfish."

Clarence was a handsome young man, with brown curly hair and large brown eyes. He was about five nine with a stocky build. His friends called him Brother, and most of the town people called him Bum.

It did not take Clarence long to get to the railroad station where he found Isom. Isom had already hopped the train to go to Louisiana to buy alcohol and was just getting off when Leonard walked into the station. When Isom stepped off the train, it was not hard to tell that he had already been drinking. He handed an open bottle to Clarence, who took a couple of swigs, and the two started walking toward the center of town. On the way, they met the police magistrate, A. A. Stein. Clarence shouted, "I was told that it was you who accused me of hollerin' and cussin' on the railroad tracks last night."

Stein replied, "I heard it was you."

Clarence glared at him and snarled, "You're a liar, and I can whip you on less grounds than you can stand on." Stein just shook his head and walked away. He knew that Clarence and Isom were drinking and that probably meant trouble.

Clarence and Isom walked on toward the downtown area, where they met a young man named Rue Emert. Clarence tripped Emert and a somewhat playful scuffle followed, during which Emert's hat was knocked off. Emert picked up his hat and remarked to Clarence, "You better watch out or that cop Witwer is goin' to get you."

Deeds replied, "That cop ain't man enough to take me in."

As Charlie approached the downtown area headed to pick up his mail, he looked around and saw that there were quite a few people still going in and out of the stores even though it was late in the afternoon. The stores would be closing soon, so everyone was busy getting what they needed for the rest of the weekend.

As he headed to Patterson's store, where the post office box was, Charlie noticed that Isom Leonard, Clarence "Bum" Deeds, and a couple of their friends were hanging around in front of the store. He also took note of the whiskey bottles they had in their hands. He squinted his eyes to see better and was sure that one of them was standing over to the side of the steps urinating.

As Charlie got close enough for them to hear, he spoke in a gruff voice, "Dammit, ain't ya got a lick o' sense. There's women an' kids walkin' 'round here. If ya have ta take a piss, at least go 'round behind a buildin'."

Upon hearing Charlie, the young man zipped up his pants and took off around the building. As Charlie walked up the steps to go into Patterson's Store, Deeds and Leonard began cussing and talking loudly that they "were goin' ta git Charlie and the mayor before morning."

Charlie decided to ignore Deeds and Leonard and walked into the store. Several people in the store nodded at Charlie, but Charlie was aware that there was not much conversation going on. He walked up to the counter and asked for his mail. Mr. Patterson told him that he did not have any mail that day. Charlie did not start a conversation with Mr. Paterson or anyone else in the store, as he usually did. He promised Lucy and Nancy he would make a quick trip, and he wanted to get back to the house for chicken an' dumplin's!

Charlie turned and walked toward the front door of the store. As he got to the doorway, Leonard and Deeds confronted him. Charlie groaned inwardly, not wanting a confrontation tonight, particularly with them. Not tonight of all nights! All he wanted to do was go home for a peaceful evening and a nice pot of chicken and dumplings with his family. He figured that one of them had been to Missouri to buy liquor, and all of them were into the "fightin' whiskey" again. This had been going on ever since he had taken over as the village marshal, and it looked like tonight would be no different. He thought that if he simply ignored them, they would go on and not cause too much trouble.

As Charlie walked out the front door, Leonard and Deeds approached him. With a sneer on his face, Leonard yelled, "You ain't big enough to take me to jail." He lowered his voice so that no one but Charlie could clearly hear him and said, "We might just take you down to the railroad tracks and throw your ass under a train."

Charlie did not want to arrest Leonard or anyone that night, and was hoping he could avoid any confrontations. He knew his brothers were at the house and could not help him; all he wanted to do was to get home to his family. Regardless, Charlie knew it was his responsibility to take care of violence in the streets. And tonight that meant arresting Deeds and Leonard.

As Charlie proceeded to accomplish his task, Deeds reached out and grabbed Charlie by the shoulder while the other thugs remained in the street. Charlie jerked his shoulder loose and tried to step around both Leonard and Deeds. Leonard and Deeds stood there for a split second, and then Leonard lunged at Charlie. As he did this, Charlie reached over Leonard's shoulder and struck Deeds with his cane. As Charlie struck the blow, he was surprised that the cane broke.

Enraged by the blow, Deeds again grabbed Charlie and threw him against the front of the building. They scuffled along the storefront, and as they did, Deeds bit down on Charlie's ear.

Charlie knew there were people close by in the street and in the store. He began yelling, "Somebody help me!" hoping that someone in the crowd that was beginning to gather would help him. No one made a move in the direction of the two grappling men. Most of the bystanders were afraid of Deeds and Leonard, and the gang that followed them around. Leonard and two other gang members formed a barrier between Charlie and Deeds and the bystanders

As Deeds and Charlie continued to struggle, they fell to the sidewalk. Deeds fell on top of Charlie when they landed, and Deeds once again began attempting to bite Charlie's ear. Both men were about the same age, but Deeds was about thirty pounds heavier than Charlie. Charlie was a strong man but was unable to get loose from the hold Deeds had on him.

As they grappled with each other, Charlie gathered all the strength he had and finally pushed Deeds off. In their struggle, the scuffle had taken them down the walk close to the front of the Phoenix Hotel. Charlie reached out for the doorframe and grabbed it, trying to pull himself up and away from Deeds. Still, no one in the crowd that stood watching moved to come to Charlie's aid or tried to break up the fight.

In a split second, and fearing for his life, Charlie reached for the pistol that was in his hip pocket. Barely getting the pistol out of his pocket, but unable to raise it and get away from Deeds, he put it against Deeds' right leg and pulled the trigger. Deeds was still holding onto Charlie, still trying to bite his ear and still did not let go of Charlie, even after he had been shot in the leg. Charlie moved the pistol up on Deeds' body and pulled the trigger again. This time the bullet struck Deeds in the abdomen. Deeds let go of Charlie, threw his hands into the air, and screamed while he stumbled backward, falling into the street. Within minutes, Clarence "Bum" Deeds was lying dead in the street. March 6, 1915, was a fateful day, never to be forgotten by Charlie Witwer or his family.

CHAPTER 34

Call for Support

Everyone was stunned and it took several seconds for the events that had taken place to register in their minds. After a few seconds with Deeds crumpled on the ground, several of his friends, including Isom Leonard, began moving toward Charlie. Charlie still had the gun in his hand and raised it toward those who were approaching. Seeing the gun raised toward them, everyone backed away as Charlie turned and ran into the hotel. Charlie knew there was a telephone on the wall in the hotel lobby and headed straight for it. More people started gathering in the street, but no one followed him into the hotel. The events that had taken place whirled through Charlie's mind. He could not seem to make sense of any of it! He knew he needed help, and the first person that came to his mind was Sheriff Edwards. He thought Sheriff Edwards would be at home since it was Saturday night and close to suppertime.

Charlie and Sheriff Edwards had become good friends since Edwards had been elected sheriff of Greene County just a couple of months before. Charlie had called him on several occasions, so he knew the phone number. Edwards had told Charlie on more than one occasion that if he ever needed help, just to call him.

Charlie grabbed his handkerchief out of his pocket and wrapped it around his ear. He tried to catch his breath as he cranked the phone to get the operator and watched out the hotel door. He gave the number to the operator and listened to the ringing of the phone at the Edwards residence. It seemed like an eternity before he heard a voice. The sheriff's wife, Delia, finally answered it and Charlie asked to speak to Edwards.

"Jesse is in Pearl with Doc Thurman. Can I give him a message when he comes home?"

"This is Charlie Witwer in Hillview. I just shot Bum Deeds an' I think I killed 'im. Do ya know if I can reach 'im in Pearl? Things are gittin' real bad here, an' I need help."

Delia replied, "You can try Dr. Thurman's number. He's probably there."

Charlie pulled out the stubby pencil he always carried in his shirt pocket and scratched Dr. Thurman's number on the wall. He knew the operator would be listening in and told her to ring the number for him. He also knew that the news of the shooting would be traveling fast. Nothing was a secret if it was discussed on a party line with an operator listening in! News traveled fast as lightning.

When Dr. Thurman answered his telephone, before he could say more than hello, Charlie yelled, "I need ta speak ta Sheriff Edwards. This is an emergency."

After a few seconds, Charlie heard Sheriff Edwards' voice, and he rushed to say, "This is Charlie Witwer. I got a serious problem over here in Hillview. Bum Deeds an' Isom Leonard attacked me at the post office. Deeds was tryin' ta kill me. I yelled for somebody ta help me but nobody helped. I shot Deeds, an' I think I killed 'im. I think all hell's goin' ta break loose, an' I'm goin' ta need all the help I can git. How quick can ya git over here?"

Sheriff Edwards did not hesitate in replying to Charlie, "I'm on my way. Try to get to your house and stay there until I get there."

The sheriff and Doc Thurman left immediately in Doc Thurman's speedster motorcar and headed for Hillview as fast as they could. They took the ferry across the

Illinois River and drove along the bottom road about four miles, which took about forty-five minutes.

After hanging up the phone, Charlie headed for the back door of the hotel. People from the street had ventured up the walk to peer into the hotel, but no one entered or even approached the door. The desk clerk was afraid to move or say a word to Charlie as he ran out the back door. As Charlie came around the building in a dead run toward his house, he looked back and saw several of Deeds' friends following him, but they stayed a distance back. They knew Charlie still had his gun. He had used it once and he just might use it again! By the time Charlie reached his house, there was a large group of Deeds' friends and townsfolk following behind.

Charlie could hear them jeering and heard someone shout, "I got a rope. We'll hang the bastard."

Another voice shouted, "We're goin' to get those three no good brothers of yours too."

Charlie ran through the door and into his house yelling to his brothers, "I think I killed Deeds, an' his gang is comin' ta git us. They plan on killin' us an' the mayor too before mornin'."

Jacob Witwer was sitting in his rocking chair in the front room half asleep and jumped up as Charlie threw the door open. Nancy, Liz, and Lucy came running to the front room from the kitchen, where they had been waiting for everyone to have supper. The minute Charlie saw his mother come out of the kitchen, he remembered chiding her about "havin' one of her feelin's."

Lucy saw Charlie and gasp, "What happened? Ya got blood all over yer shirt an' the side o' yer face. What happened ta yer ear?"

Charlie reached up to feel his ear where Deeds had tried to bite it several times and replied, "Deeds tried ta bite it off. Those bastards were drinkin' an' hangin' around in front o' the post office. When I came out, they tried ta jump me an' kill me. I shot Bum Deeds."

By this time, everyone was in the front room. They could hear the ruckus going on in front of the house in the street. One by one Jim, Ernest and Dick cautiously looked out the window to see if they could tell who was in the crowd and what they were doing. After seeing how many had gathered and listening to the shouting, Jim decided to barricade the front door with a chair. Charlie walked to the kitchen with Nancy where he took off his shirt while she poured a pan of water to clean the blood off his face. As he took his shirt off, Nancy noticed blood on his pants near his belt buckle and said, "Is yer belly bleedin'?"

"No, that's probably Bum Deeds' blood."

Lucy, so frightened she was shaking, tried to wring out the rag to clean off the blood. She groaned, "I knew this was goin' ta happen. That gang outside is goin' ta kill us all."

Dick walked into the kitchen about that time and said, "We ain't goin' ta let that happen."

CHAPTER 35

The Standoff

As Charlie was getting cleaned up, the three brothers gathered all of the guns and ammunition they had. Lucy and Nancy hurriedly cleared off the kitchen table and sat the bowls on the cabinet top. No one was thinking about that pot of chicken and dumplings sitting on the stove. Liz stood in the corner sobbing as she watched the guns and ammunition being brought to the kitchen table.

Dick grabbed a .22 rifle, loaded it, removed the chair from under the door handle of the front door, and slowly opened the door. As he walked onto the porch, the crowd started to jeer, but he raised his rifle in the air and shouted, "The first one of ya that comes any nearer ta this house will be joinin' Deeds in hell." The crowd got very quiet. Dick listened carefully to see if he could hear any pistols or rifles being cocked by someone who was carrying a gun. As he scanned the crowd, he could feel the anger radiating as they began to cuss and threaten to kill all of the Witwer brothers.

Dick slowly backed into the house and quickly shut the door, barricading it once again. It was beginning to get dark as people stood around in the street. After a short while, the crowd started to diminish as some of the townsfolk left. There was still a small crowd milling around in the street, but the yelling had died down a little. As Charlie peered out from the edge of the window, he thought he recognized Leonard and some of the gang members. There were a few of the townsfolk still meandering around, but he could not tell who they were. A few were waving something in the air. That something looked like firearms of some kind. One of them had a rope, waved it in the air, and started chanting, "Let's hang that son of a bitch." Occasionally, the thud of rocks hitting the front of the house could be heard, and a small one burst through a windowpane in the front room. Glass spewed into the wooden floor, letting the cool night air drift in along with the taunts that were being yelled.

The window being broken sent Lucy, Liz and Nancy into a state of panic. They ran to one of the bedrooms and crouched down in the dark listening to the shouts and noise. Jacob hovered in the hall listening to his sons. The shouting did not seem to be dying down much, and it seemed like hours had passed, although it was only minutes. They could not see each other's faces in the darkened rooms but knew that fear was in all of their eyes and etched on their faces. There was no conversation other than Nancy mumbling, "I knew somethin' bad was goin' ta happen. I told Charlie not ta go ta town."

After a few minutes, Lucy crawled along the floor and found Charlie looking out the window in the front room. "Charlie," she said, "We gotta git ya outta here, an' I think I got an idea."

"How the hell 're we gonna git through that crowd, Lucy. Those hoodlums 're out fer blood."

"The neighbor behind us has bales o' hay in his wagon. Ya remember every night right after suppertime, he hauls 'em over ta his cow barn over by the old schoolhouse. I know he's got his team hooked up, 'cause he always does by this time. We could hide ya under those bales o' hay, an' he could drive ya outta here. They won't think nothin' o' him drivin' his wagon ta his barn."

Dick, who sometimes had more confidence than sense, seemed to be enjoying what was going on. He overheard what Lucy was telling Charlie and turned to say, "That might not be a bad idea. If I walk out on the porch with Jim's double barrel 12-gauge shotgun an' load it, that might git their attention. Jim an' Ernest can stand in the doorway with a gun, an' it might distract 'em long 'nough fer Lucy's plan ta work."

By this time, they were all paying less attention to those in front of the house and more attention to what was being said. Ernest said, "Dick, I think yer nuts. If ya walk out there, ya just might git shot. And then there'll be a war, an' we might be the losers! There's more o' them than there is o' us."

Dick looked at him. "Ya got a better idea? I'm not goin' ta shoot anybody. I just want 'em ta know we mean business. We gotta git Charlie outta here now! It's him they want ta string up the most. They might all go home if they think Charlie's done slipped out."

Jacob had not said much up to this point but felt that he needed to express his opinion. "Why don't we try ta do what Lucy says an' git Charlie down ta the jail? A couple of ya can slip down there as soon as it gits good an' dark. There's bars on the windows an' a good lock on the door. The rest of us can wait fer Sheriff Edwards ta git here."

Charlie knew that most of the gang members had been drinking and probably still had their whiskey bottles with them. The longer they were out there drinking, the more out of control things were likely to get. He knew he had to figure out some way to keep Lucy, Nancy, Liz, and Jacob safe. After thinking about Lucy's plan for a couple of minutes and considering what Jacob had said, he turned to all of them and said, "I cain't think of a better plan so let's try it. Lucy needs ta go out the back way an' git over ta the neighbor's before he takes off. She can see if he'll drive me outta here. I'll watch out the back door ta see if she motions fer me ta come."

As Lucy grabbed her coat and slipped out the back door, she saw the neighbor standing on his back porch. She was thankful he had not yet left. She scurried across the backyard and up onto his back porch as quickly as she could. Charlie hunched down at the back door peering out through the screen door watching Lucy. He could see both heads nodding as the two stood on the porch while Lucy pointed to the wagon full of bales of hay. It did not take long before Lucy was motioning for him to run for the wagon.

Dick heard the screech of the back screen door as Charlie yelled that he was headed to the wagon. Dick yanked up Jim's double-barreled shotgun and a pocketful of shells and walked through the front door. Ernest and Jim followed him out onto the porch and stood a few feet apart in the shadows, holding their hunting pistols down at their side. As the crowd watched a figure come out the door and then saw Dick raise the shotgun, a hush swept over those that were still milling about in the street. A few backed away, but several of them did not move. As Dick had hoped, the crowd was focused on what he was doing and was not aware of the activity in the back of the house.

Charlie ran to the wagon as the neighbor pulled one bale of hay off. He quickly jumped into the wagon, scooting between the bales. The neighbor threw an old horse blanket on top of Charlie and climbed up onto the driver's bench. He moved slowly, just as he did every night. He picked up the reigns and sat down on the wooden seat. He let the brake off the wagon and started driving the team of horses down the side street toward Railroad Street. He barely glanced over at the crowd as he passed the corner because he did not want to draw attention to himself. All eyes from the crowd were still on Dick standing on the front porch with the shotgun, so they paid little attention to the wagon rolling down the street.

CHAPTER 36

Sheriff Edwards

As the wagon rolled down the side street past the crowd, Doc Thurman and Sheriff Edwards were speeding up the street toward the Witwer house. As they rolled up behind the crowd, Doc Thurman cut the engine off on the car. Sheriff Edwards jumped out, shoved his way through those standing in the street while yelling at them to stand back. As he ran up the steps onto the front porch, Doc Thurman sat in the car. Not everyone in the crowd knew Sheriff Edwards so they were wondering who this man was. When Sheriff Edwards stepped up on the porch and saw Dick standing with his shotgun, he growled at Dick, "Put that damn thing down before somebody else gets killed and that crowd really goes crazy."

Dick took a step backward as he lowered the shotgun and opened the screened door so he could stand in the doorway. Sheriff Edwards stood on the porch with his back to the crowd talking to Dick, Jim, and Ernest.

Dick quietly explained, "We just got Charlie outta here. Charlie was in the back o' that wagon that just went down the street. He's goin' down ta the jail an' lockin' himself in. One of us is goin' ta go down as soon as it gits good an' dark."

Sheriff Edwards just shook his head in disbelief at what had just taken place. The sheriff was a large, imposing individual with a booming voice. He turned to the crowd and shouted to them that Charlie was not in the house. He told them he knew where Charlie was and that he was the sheriff of Greene County and had the authority to take Charlie into custody. He reminded the crowd that there were three women in the house plus an elderly man. If any harm came to anybody in the Witwer household, he personally would see to it that whoever was responsible would be arrested and sent away for a long time.

As Sheriff Edwards spoke, no one in the crowd made any noise or even shuffled their feet. There was dead silence. The sheriff stood on the porch, not making a move or saying another word. As he stood and stared at them for several minutes, the crowd began to thin out. After a few minutes, only a few of the townsfolk were still hanging around with Leonard and his friends. Someone in the crowd yelled out, "We'll find 'im before the night's over and when we do…"

Jim said to Sheriff Edwards, "Isom Leonard is the one that was yelling that threat, and probably they all been drinkin' all afternoon."

Sheriff Edwards looked out into the thinning crowd and was able to see Leonard standing a little in front of the rest. He pointed his finger directly at him and said, "That kind of talk will get you behind bars real quick. One more comment like that outta anyone, and you'll be spending time in my jail. I'm going in the house now, and I'm going to walk back out onto this porch in five minutes. When I come back out, I don't want to see one person out there."

Sheriff Edwards opened the screen door and walked into the house. As he stood peering out into the darkness, he could see that the people were beginning to break into small groups and amble off. He had a good idea which ones were the troublemakers. He was sure that some of them, like Isom Leonard, had nasty tempers, especially when there was drinking going on. He needed to get this whole situation calmed down before somebody else was shot!

He turned to the Witwer family and said, "I'm going to the jail to see Charlie, but I'm going to wait a few minutes for the streets to clear out. I want all of you to stay put in the house with the doors locked and keep the lamps turned down. Stay away from the windows. Charlie is not safe as long as he's in Hillview, so I'm thinking about taking him to the jail in Carrollton."

Nobody had much to say for the next few minutes. What could they say? They were all at a total loss as to what might take place next or what to do next. When Sheriff Edwards was confident that the mob was not going to cause any more trouble, he walked out of the house and to the car where Doc Thurman was still waiting.

Liz had been so frightened all evening, all she could do was cry rivers of tears streaming down her cheeks. She was glad to hear the sheriff tell Dick, along with Earnest and Jim, to stay in the house. She had been almost hysterical when Dick went out onto the front porch with the shotgun. Lucy, Nancy, and Jacob nodded in agreement with the sheriff when he said he thought he would take Charlie to the jail in Carrollton where he would be safe from Leonard and the gang. They all wanted Charlie far away from Hillview.

Doc Thurman had been sitting in his car behind the crowd while Sheriff Edwards was with the Witwer family, observing what was taking place. When the sheriff got back to the car, he drove the sheriff to the jail and parked in the back, a couple of buildings away from the jail. Sheriff Edwards quickly walked around the buildings and up to the door of the jail. He rapped on it as he identified himself and called out Charlie's name. Charlie recognized the sheriff's voice and quickly unlocked the door. Sheriff Edwards stepped in as quickly as he could, shut the door, and stood for a moment until his eyes adjusted to the darkness.

"Charlie, what in tarnation happened today?"

Standing in the dark room, Charlie took a deep breath and said, “I tried ta git away from ’im, but he just kept comin’ at me. I yelled out fer some help but nobody’d do anythin’. He threw me down, got on top o’ me an’ kept tryin’ ta bite my ear off.” Charlie pointed to his bloody, swollen ear. “Bum Deeds threatened ta kill me right then an’ there. I’m sure several people heard ’im say that. He an' those buddies o' his was drinkin’. I got out from under ’im an’ tried ta git up. I kept yellin’ fer help. He got me against the wall an' that’s when I pulled my gun out an’ shot ’im in the leg. That didn’t stop ’im so I shot ’im in the gut. I told ya there's been all kind o’ talk that he was goin’ ta take care o’ me an’ the mayor.”

Sheriff Edwards listened intently as Charlie told his story. After a few moments, Sheriff Edwards scratched his head and said, “If it happened like you told me, it sounds like self-defense, but I’m not a judge and jury. When that gang figures out that you’re in this little jail, they’ll burn it down if they have to to get to you. Even if they don’t do that, that door won’t hold ’em out if there’s enough of them. I’m going to arrest you and take you to the Greene County Jail in Carrollton. It’s more for your own protection than anything else. Why don’t you give me that pistol you have? When this is all over, I’ll give it back to you.”

Reluctantly, Charlie unloaded the pistol and handed it over to Sheriff Edwards. Charlie trusted the sheriff and said, “I’ll go ta Carrollton with ya, but my family needs ta be told what the plan is.”

Sheriff Edwards assured Charlie that he had told his family of his plan, and they had agreed that it was better than Charlie staying in Hillview.

The sheriff told Charlie to stay put. “I am going to have a deputy take you to Carrollton, so when he drives up in front of the jail, you get in the car with him. It’ll be a little while before he gets here. I can’t use a phone to call him because those operators tell everything they hear. The doors of this jail will be torn off before I even get out of town if I use the phone. I'll have to go to his house."

Charlie kept watch at the window, all the time wondering what was going on with his family and wondering if Leonard and his gang would come looking for him at the jail. He knew that Lucy would be in a state of high anxiety but he had to stay in that jail.

It seemed like a lifetime before he heard the rumble of a car. It was quite late, and he figured that nobody else would be out in their car at this hour. It had to be Sheriff Edwards' deputy. He peaked out the window, his eyes squinting to focus to see the car and the driver. With his heart pounding, he jerked the jail door open, ran across the walk, quickly jumped into the car and crouched down. He sure hoped he had jumped into the right car! The deputy driving did not waste any time in stomping on the gas pedal, and they roared out of town. Not much conversation passed between the two of them as they drove to Carrollton. Charlie was thankful for that. His mind was in such turmoil that he could hardly put a coherent sentence together.

When they arrived at the Carrollton jail, it was after midnight. As they walked in, a sense of doom settled over Charlie. He felt as though he had lost control of his life, and it was definitely not headed in the right direction! The deputy opened the door to the cell, and Charlie hesitantly walked in. As that door made the familiar clinking sound as it was shut and locked, Charlie wondered just how many nights he would be spending behind those bars. He had heard that sound many times, but he had always been the one on the other side of the door, holding the key. His heart lurched, and a wave of nausea overtook him, as he stood like a statue unable to take another step.

Sheriff Edwards realized the situation in Hillview was volatile, and he needed to get some help there as soon as possible. He knew that for a long time, there had been a rowdy element in Hillview, and they did not like anyone who tried to restore order in the village. Since taking office in January, Sheriff Edwards had heard rumors that some of the townsfolk did not think that Charlie and his deputies were "tactful" in their efforts to enforce the law. He had even heard talk that a number of citizens had signed a petition to have Charlie removed as the village marshal. Evidently, neither the mayor nor the council had taken any action. He did not know if these rumors contained any truth or not. Based on all of the talk, though, he had to assume that Charlie and his brothers had aroused a considerable amount of antagonism in the village. It was not his place to take sides but to simply uphold the law.

CHAPTER 37

The Lockdown

Sheriff Edwards quickly made the decision to go back and stay the night in Hillview just to make sure everything stayed quiet. Then he would assign Deputy Sheriff Markum to spend a few days in Hillview. Sheriff Edwards wanted the word to spread to everyone in town that just because the town had no village marshal, he, as the county sheriff, would take care of the law enforcement. He knew he would have to drop by the Witwer house in the morning to let them know that Charlie was safe in custody in the Greene County Jail. He was sure they were very worried and anxious to hear from him.

It was not long after the shooting incident that one of the townsfolk banged on Mayor Coates' door and told him that Charlie had shot and killed Clarence "Bum" Deeds. When Mayor Coates heard about the shooting and that the talk was that the gang was "going to get the mayor and the village marshal before sunrise," it did not take him long to decide what to do. He loaded his family in his car and quickly headed out of town to safety. When his life was being threatened, he was not taking any chances by staying in Hillview!

The body of Clarence "Bum" Deeds was carried into Patterson's Store after the shooting incident. As the news traveled around the town, many residents left whatever they were doing and began gathering in and around the store trying to find out more about what had happened. The telephone operator and those listening in on the party line spread the news in a hurry! The stories were not always the same as the information passed among the people.

When Deputy Coroner T. H. Carmody was told about the shooting, he immediately left his house and went to Patterson's Store to examine the body. It was getting late in the evening, but he knew the body had to be moved from the store. He then arranged with the Deeds' family to have him transferred to a funeral home in White Hall.

Late in the evening, the deputy coroner impaneled a jury of eleven men and one woman to serve on the coroner's jury. The hearing was held at the Phoenix Hotel as soon as the jury was appointed. Those who served on the jury were Samuel Mundy, Edward Hoskins, C. R. Augie, Ernest L. Ford, Fred Gibler, F. H. Patterson, Isham Leonard, Beasley Bateman, Walter Reed, Ernest Thomas, Clarence Turner, and Anna Scott.

It was believed that more than one of the jurors was present at the time of the shooting. It was also rumored that more than one of them was a friend of Clarence "Bum" Deeds. Apparently, Isham Leonard was a relative of Isom Leonard, who was involved in the scuffle at the time of the shooting. F. H. Patterson was the owner of the store and post office where the altercation started. Those who were present at the shooting gave conflicting statements and told many different versions about what took place between Deeds and Marshal Charlie. This made it difficult to ascertain the facts. For the most part, though, they agreed that the village marshal tried to avoid the altercation.

The verdict handed down by the coroner's jury late that evening was neutral in its nature. It stated, "Clarence Deeds died from a gunshot wound from a pistol in the hands of Village Marshal Charles R. Witwer." This verdict did not affix any blame on Charlie, nor did it vindicate him.

Of course, neither Charlie nor his family knew what was taking place, and they had no way of finding out.

After the inquest, those on the jury left the store and quickly headed home. It did not take long for the crowd to dissipate. The streets of Hillview looked like those of a ghost town for the rest of the weekend. Most of the residents were quite shocked at what had happened and were afraid to be out and about the town, unless they absolutely had to be. Church was about the only place anyone went, and the only topic of conversation was about the Saturday night shooting.

CHAPTER 38

The Flight from Hillview

Once Charlie's family received the information from Sheriff Edwards that Charlie had been taken safely to the Greene County Jail, needless to say, they were greatly relieved. They were still in a state of turmoil, but that news helped calm their nerves a little. Jim, Ernest, and Dick agreed they had to get out of Hillview—and get out fast! They were concerned for themselves, but they were even more concerned that no harm come to Lucy, Liz, Nancy, and Jacob. Getting the four of them out of Hillview posed a problem. Where would they go? How would they get them out? There were no ready answers.

Old Jacob told his sons that they should "stand and fight"—a throwback phrase from his days in the Civil War—but Jim and Ernest knew that the situation was far too volatile for that kind of action, particularly with three women in the house. Dick, who was always ready for fight, sided with Jacob, but nobody else agreed with him or paid much attention to his comments. Nancy told Jacob, "It just ain't worth it." Lucy, of course, was worried sick about Charlie. She tried to be strong in front of Liz, but her stomach churned and her hands shook as she listened to the three brothers trying to figure out what to do. Liz did little more than stand in the hall doorway and wring her hands with tears running in streams down her face. Lucy and Liz were still young women and had not seen this type of violence.

Ernest had been spending quite a lot of time with the Milby family in New Berlin. He had seen their brother, Frank, who lived in Springfield, on several occasions when he was in New Berlin. He knew Frank would help them find a place to stay somewhere, if they could all just get out of Hillview.

Early the next morning before sunrise, after a sleepless night, when he thought there would be few people on the streets, Ernest slipped down to the jail and asked the sheriff if he could use the telephone to call his brother. The telephone had only been installed a few months earlier, and Ernest certainly was glad. He worried that the operator would be listening in, but he had to take that chance. Before he gave the operator the number, Sheriff Edwards took the phone, identified himself and said, "Whoever is listening had better not repeat anything that is being said during this call, or they will have to answer to me." Ernest felt a sense of relief as the sheriff handed the phone back to him. Ernest was sure that Frank would be at home this early in the morning.

When Frank answered, Ernest hastily told him what had happened. It did not take Frank long to tell him to get Lucy, Liz, Jacob, and Nancy on the earliest train out of Hillview the next morning and for them to get off in Jacksonville. He assured Ernest he would find some place for them to stay and would meet them at the train station. Ernest quickly told Sheriff Edwards what the plan was.

As daylight was beginning to break, Ernest hurried back to the house to tell the rest of the family about his conversation with Frank. All of them were somewhat relieved, but apprehensive. There were no objections to the plan, though, because no one else had a better one. Jacob, Nancy, Liz and Lucy spent the day gathering what they were going to take on the train, while one of the brothers kept an eye on the street. The house sat on a hill, so it was easy to see if anyone was approaching. There was not much conversation throughout the day. They were still in a state of shock with what had taken place the night before. All of Lucy's thoughts were about what might happen to Charlie. She was so preoccupied with her thoughts, she kept forgetting what she was doing.

After another restless night, Lucy, Liz, Nancy, and Jacob boarded the first early morning train on Monday that was traveling east out of Hillview. All of them left the house with trepidation, hoping there would not be any trouble. Sheriff Edwards had posted a deputy at the train station just in case the family did try to carry out the plan that Ernest had informed him of.

Liz, Lucy, Nancy, and Jacob had packed as much as they could carry. The bags were loaded into the Model T in the early morning darkness shortly before it was time to leave. It was decided that Ernest should drive the car to the station while the other two stayed at the house. Ernest had been gone from Hillview quite a bit, and there did not seem to be as much animosity toward him as there was toward Jim and Dick.

When it was time to go, Lucy, Liz, and Nancy crowded into the backseat, almost sitting on top of each other, while Jacob sat in the front with Ernest. Leaving brought on another round of sobs and tears from Liz. She did not want to leave Dick and had clung to him until Lucy made her get into the car. Lucy was almost in a state of panic, but she knew she had to stay in control. The bags were piled on top of the ladies' laps, and Jacob scrunched the rest around him in the front. Since their trek to the train station was early in the morning before the sun came up, they did not see any people on the street. It was a short ride, so they did not have to worry about getting too cold in the early morning frosty air. There were very few people in the station this early in the morning. Seeing the deputy posted at the door eased their minds, and they felt safer.

It was barely light outside when the early morning train pulled out of the station, and they could see the silhouettes of the buildings and houses of the town they had called home for many months. As they looked out the dirt-streaked train windows, they wondered how this chapter of their lives was going to end. Lucy wanted desperately to see Charlie, but the train would not be going through Carrollton. She did not know when she would see her husband again, or what was going to happen to him. Jacob and Nancy did not know when they would be seeing their oldest son and were concerned about the safety of their three sons left in Hillview. Liz was numb with fear, not only for herself, but for Dick as well. Their worries were so great that they hardly thought about what was going to happen to them when they got off that train in Jacksonville.

As Frank had promised, he and his wife were waiting anxiously on the platform at the Jacksonville train station. Even though he had only one day to find a place for them to live, he had found a house for them to move into. It seemed like a miracle. The house was located at 850 West Lafayette in Jacksonville, Illinois. Frank and his wife, Ethel, stood on the platform, eager to see his parents, Jacob and Nancy. They did not know Lucy and Liz very well having only met them one time, but they were considered family now that they had married Charlie and Dick. Frank wished that seeing everyone was under better circumstances, but he was thankful that all of them had gotten out of Hillview and traveled safely to Jacksonville. Every time Ernest had seen Frank in the past few weeks, he had told Frank of the troubles in Hillview. Frank was still shocked when he heard about the shooting and the danger the family was in if they stayed in Hillview.

To get everyone to the house with their bags and sacks, Frank had to make two trips from the train station. A burden was lifted from everyone's shoulders when they saw their new home—they had a place to live! If the previous couple of days had not been such stressful ones, they would have been even more excited. No one cared what the house looked like or what was in the house. They were just glad to have a safe place to come to after what they had been through since the shooting had occurred.

Even though the house did not look quite as big as the house in Hillview, everyone was elated to have a place to once again call home. As they climbed out of the car, they stood on the curb looking at a two-story house facing a brick-paved street.It had windows looking out onto the small front porch. As they explored the house, they saw that the rooms were large with lots of windows. The house had an indoor well pump and floors that did not squeak! It was sparsely furnished, but all of the furniture was in good shape. At least the kitchen table was not scarred like the one they had had in Hillview, and the icebox did not have a broken leg.

Frank told them that the house was less than two blocks from a well-supplied grocery store with fresh bread and even had a butcher shop in it. As they walked into the house, Nancy looked at Jacob and said, “I have a good feelin’ ’bout this place.” That statement made Jacob give her a quick little hug.

Having lived with Nancy and her premonitions for the past few months, hearing her words buoyed Lucy and Liz’s spirits. Lucy and Liz kept walking around peeking into every closet and cabinet and were rather awestruck—they were going to have running water inside the house! A fresh batch of tears came to their eyes. Frank did not know if they were crying because they were sad or because they were happy.

CHAPTER 39

Witwer Brothers Depart Hillview

As soon as Lucy, Liz, Nancy and Jacob were safely on the train and it had pulled out of the station, Ernest drove back to the house. He did not want to spend any more time on the streets than was necessary, nor did he want to encounter anyone that might cause trouble. There would be no trip to Mrs. Greene's today!

When Jim and Dick were not taking their turns watching out the front window the day before, they had packed as much as they could. By the time Ernest got back from the train station, they were ready to load the Model T and head to Jacksonville. They had been in Hillview for a little less than one and a half years, and it had been a tumultuous time. There was a great deal of remorse about the way they were leaving, but knew they did not have a choice. They felt a sense of relief that they were soon going to be on their way.

Everyone in Sheriff Edwards' office knew they were leaving. The brothers had made it clear that they were leaving armed and would do whatever was necessary to make it out of town unharmed. The sheriff was more than glad to see them go. He knew that as long as any of the Witwers were in Hillview, there was a good possibility that trouble would erupt, and it just might be serious trouble. He had enough to do with his own job without taking on the trouble in Hillview, but under the circumstances, he did not have much choice.

It did not take long for the Model T to be loaded. As Dick and Ernest jumped in, Jim turned the crank to get it started. The sun had come up but it was still early, and they were hoping there would not be many people on the streets as they left. The fellows that caused trouble never seemed to hit the streets until the afternoon, so they were hoping it would be the same today. Without the gangs to start trouble, they did not think that any of the townsfolk would do much other than maybe hurl verbal insults at them. Insults they could take. They just did not want to engage in any kind of altercations as they rolled out of Hillview, and they did not intend to ever return!

The mood was somber as they sped out of town. Jim drove as fast as he could, taking the corners so fast that Dick and Ernest had a hard time staying upright in their seats. The March air was cold, and they pulled their coats around themselves tightly. They let out sighs of relief once they hit the edge of Hillview without encountering any trouble. Jim thought his body was tense because of the cold but when Hillview was in the rear view mirror, he realized the tension came from the flight out of town. They felt like they were being run out of town but did not want to admit that to each other. When they had moved to Hillview, they had done so with the anticipation of a new job and a new life. Leaving under these circumstances did not sit well with any of them.

Jim continued driving toward Jacksonville as fast as he could make the Model T go. He hit a couple of potholes so hard that Ernest and Dick thought their teeth would rattle. Dick poked Jim on the shoulder and hollered, "At least Lucy an' Liz are happy ta be outta Hillview, an' Mom an' Dad 're safe in Jacksonville. Now all we gotta do is git Charlie outta jail."

Jim had a frown on his face because he knew what Dick was thinking about. "We ain't goin' ta do nothin' crazy, so jus' ferget it. Charlie shot Deeds in self-defense, an' the jury will find 'im not guilty if he has ta go ta trial. We don't need anybody else in jail."

Ernest turned to Dick and said, "I agree with Jim. The only way we're goin' ta git Charlie outta jail is if they set bond fer his release, an' if we kin raise the money."

Ernest, who had plans to marry Bertha Milby, had planned to leave Hillview anyway, so he felt no loss as they drove out of town. He wanted to work on the Milby farm, or some other farm near New Berlin. He asked Jim to take him to the Milby farm after stopping to see everyone in Jacksonville. Ernest was looking forward to a new life in New Berlin.

Neither Jim nor Dick could even guess at what their future held. Their departure from Hillview had been so quick and hectic that neither of them had given much thought to what they were going to do when they arrived in Jacksonville, nor did they know anything about Jacksonville. They just knew that they would be starting over once again in a new town. This was a concern to them but they knew they had no choice. They could not depend on Jacob to support the family, and Charlie was in jail, so they knew it was up to them to figure it all out. Even though these thoughts weighed heavily on their minds, most of their thoughts as they drove along were about Charlie and what might happen to him.

CHAPTER 40

A Village Divided

When Charlie and his brothers agreed to move to Hillview and take the positions in law enforcement, they were not going into the situation blindly. The altercation in the saloon, as they were traveling through Hillview before Charlie was offered the position, gave them a good idea of what they might be confronted with. They knew the community had been rampant with lawlessness and that there were several unexplained deaths. They had made some headway in quelling the nightly altercations and the harassment of the townspeople, but it was not enough. Some of the residents agreed with the way Charlie and his brothers handled the lawlessness, and others thought they were too harsh. Before, during, and after the shooting, emotions in the village of Hillview ran high. After the shooting, there was even more division within the town, and the rumors were rampant.

After the shooting, the headlines of the Carrollton newspaper, the *Carrollton Patriot*, read, "Another Killing in Hillview! When Is the Violence Going to Stop?"

Neither the village officials nor the residents liked to see headlines like this about their community. Now, they had no village marshal, and they were not sure where their mayor was!

On Monday, as the Witwer family was on its way to Jacksonville, Mayor Coates traveled from his hiding place to Carrollton to have a conference with Sheriff Edwards.

During that meeting, official steps were taken to remove Charlie as the village marshal, thereby removing the three brothers as the deputies. At that time, the biggest concerns of Mayor Coates were the safety of his family and how any semblance of peace was going to be restored to Hillview. Mayor Coates had not forgotten the threats that had been made against his life. He was not sure he wanted to return to Hillview.

Sheriff Edwards explained to the mayor that he had ordered at least one deputy to be in Hillview at all times until the streets were calm. The only problem was that they were not allowed to arrest or incarcerate anyone in the Hillview jail, including any of the troublemakers. It was not long before the gangs began to roam and rule the streets again now that Marshal Charlie and his deputies were gone. There was no limit as to how much trouble the troublemakers could cause. Within a few weeks, many of the Hillview residents and business owners were thinking that maybe Marshal Charlie and his deputies were not so bad after all.

Chapter 41

A Charge of Murder!

As the gray morning light seeped through the windows of the Greene County Jail the morning after the shooting, Charlie sat on the hard cot in his cell, head in his hands, replaying the events of Saturday night over and over in his mind. How had the situation gotten out of hand so quickly? Why didn't anyone come forward to help him? Why didn't he take one of his brothers to town with him? Why didn't he listen to his mother when she asked him to stay home? There were no answers. Only unanswered questions!

He was distraught and racked with grief that he had caused the death of another man, regardless of the circumstances. He worried about Lucy and the rest of his family. These thoughts only brought more questions to his mind. Sheriff Edwards had told him that his family was going to Jacksonville but that was all he knew. Where were they going to live? How were Jim and Dick going to support the family? How was Lucy handling the situation? How hard was this move on his mom and dad? Again, only questions and no answers.

Sheriff Edwards had told Charlie what the verdict was from the coroner's jury. Charlie knew they could not keep him in that cell for very long without a formal complaint being signed. As Monday morning dawned, he wondered how long it would take before he heard if they were going to charge him with something, or if they were going to let him go. He certainly did not want to sit in that cell behind that locked door. His stomach churned as he thought about what the charge might be.

Charlie was sure that before long, a deputy would be bringing him something for breakfast, but he was not sure he could swallow a bite, even though he had not had anything to eat since Saturday noon. When they brought him a tray on Sunday morning, he sent most of the food back. His stomach was in such an uproar that just the smell of it made him feel worse. Oh, how he wished he was sitting at his kitchen table watching the sun come up and listening to the sounds of breakfast cooking on the stove. His thoughts were so muddled he thought that maybe a hot cup of strong coffee would clear his head, even if it did not do much for his stomach. Unfortunately, nothing made him feel better.

The day crept by. There was nothing for Charlie to do but sit on his cot and think. And that was not something he wanted to do. Thinking only brought on recriminations and feelings of remorse. He was glad when the evening shadows fell across his cell. He knew the night was going to be unbearable, but he had to get through it. What choice did he have?

Late on Monday morning, Charlie looked through the bars of his cell and saw Sheriff Edwards walking toward him with a grim look on his face. Charlie was not sure his legs would hold him if he stood up. As Sheriff Edwards reached into his pocket and unfolded a piece of paper, Charlie knew that a formal complaint had been handed down. Charlie walked across his cell and grabbed the bars so tightly his knuckles turned white, and said, "Do ya have somethin' ta tell me, Sheriff Edwards?"

Sheriff Edwards nodded and replied, "The police magistrate handed down a criminal complaint this morning. I'll read it to you.

"'"Charles R. Witwer committed said offense and did then and there unlawfully, willfully, and with malice aforethought kill Clarence Deeds, a human being, being there and there in the peace of the people, contrary to the form of the Statute in such case made and provided, and against the peace and dignity of the People of the State of Illinois, and therefore prays that the said Charles R. Witwer may be arrested and dealt with according to the law. That the offense of murder has been committed in said state and that said complainant has just and reasonable grounds to suspect that Charles R. Witwer is guilty of said offense of murder. Mabel Carter, Honorable Police Magistrate and Justice of the Peace."'"

Charlie was in a state of shock and his knees started to buckle. If he had not had such a tight grip on the cell bars, he was sure he would have fallen to the floor. How could he be charged with murder? His mind raced. He had shot Clarence Deeds in self-defense. He had tried to get away from Clarence Deeds. He had yelled for help. Didn't anybody understand what had happened?

Charlie was well acquainted with the law. He knew what that complaint meant. He was too distraught to say anything to Sheriff Edwards and simply shuffled back to his cot and sat down, staring at the floor. Sheriff Edwards knew it was best to give Charlie some time to get over the shock of what the complaint said. He knew that Charlie would want his family to know as soon as possible but had no idea how to contact them. He was sure they would get in contact with him just as soon as they could.

CHAPTER 42

Jail Time

Charlie was pale and shaky when Sheriff Edwards checked on him a little while later. He knew that Charlie had not eaten anything that morning, or much the day before, so he went to the restaurant across from the jail to get a hot meal for Charlie's dinner. He took it in to Charlie and encouraged him to eat something. He told Charlie that he would come back in about an hour. Sheriff Edwards had come to like Charlie in the short time he knew him and was heavyhearted to see Charlie in his jail with a charge of murder brought against him.

Before Sheriff Edwards went back to Charlie's cell to pick up the food tray, he received a phone call from Jim. As soon as Jim got to Jacksonville on Monday and he was able to find a phone, he called the sheriff to see what was going to happen to Charlie. The sheriff hated to tell Jim about the formal complaint that was filed against Charlie but knew the family needed the information. Jim was so stunned at what the sheriff told him he did little but mumble as he said he would call again after he talked to the family. Sheriff Edwards tried to make Jim understand that he could bring Lucy, or any family member, to see Charlie during certain hours, but Jim was too numb to listen and hung up the telephone.

After the conversation with Sheriff Edwards, Charlie knew he was not going to get out of that jail cell any time soon, and that there was nothing he could do about it.

He wondered how long it would be before they would formally arrest him. As he sat there, he had no idea that he was going to have to sit in that lonely jail cell for many days before the next action was taken. It was a good thing he could not see into the future!

CHAPTER 43

The Formal Complaint

On March 20, 1915, Charles R. Witwer, defendant, was formally arrested and appeared in court at a preliminary hearing. He had been in custody in the Carrollton jail since a few hours after the shooting on March 6—fourteen long days! Sheriff Edwards repeatedly told Charlie that he was safer in jail than he was out on the streets, but those words did not help Charlie, or his family, deal with the circumstances. No words could comfort any of them. Their lives were fragmented and in turmoil! Lucy was inconsolable knowing that Charlie had been arrested.

Word had spread quickly around Hillview that Charlie would be appearing at a preliminary hearing on March 20. A large contingency of Hillview residents, both witnesses to the shooting and spectators who simply wanted to be up on the news, boarded the train from Hillview early that Saturday morning. They were headed to Carrollton for the hearing at the courthouse. The courtroom was so full that spectators had to stand wherever they could find a little space.

Lucy and Jim had made a couple of trips on the train to see Charlie during the two weeks Charlie had been sitting in the Carrollton jail. Money was tight, but everyone knew it was important to both Lucy and Charlie to see each other, even under those terrible circumstances. Lucy had a difficult time seeing Charlie locked up, but wanted to spend as much time with him as she could. She just could not help but wonder why Charlie had been charged with murder. She only knew what Charlie had told her, but she knew that Charlie would not shoot a man unless it was in self-defense.

On the day of the preliminary hearing, Jim, Lucy, and Jacob piled into the Model T and drove to Carrollton, which was about thirty five miles from Jacksonville. They did not want to risk taking the train for fear that it would be late, and they would not make it to the hearing in time. It was a brisk March morning. The sun was shining in the clear, blue sky, but the mood in the car was dark and gloomy. Jacob turned to Lucy and gave her a weak smile, "Lucy, we'll git through this. We gotta be strong fer Charlie." Lucy nodded her head as she blinked back the tears in her eyes.

When they arrived at the courthouse, there was already a crowd that had gathered waiting for the doors to open. Jim, Lucy, and Jacob stayed close to the car until the doors started to open. As they hurried across the street and approached the crowd, many people stepped back a little to let them through. They were probably doing this more out of respect for Lucy and Jacob rather than Jim. The three of them walked directly up the steps, through the door and to the front of the courtroom without speaking to anyone. They took a seat in the front row with their heads held high. They wanted to make sure that Charlie saw them when he was brought into the courtroom. Jim and Jacob sat on each side of Lucy.

State's Attorney J. C. Bowman was the lead attorney for the prosecution and was assisted by H. Clay Williams of Pittsfield. Judge Thomas Henshaw of Carrollton and E. C. Knotts, district attorneys from Carlinville, were retained for the defense of Charlie. The prosecution argued to have Charlie held without bond, but the defense attorneys argued that he fired in self-defense while performing his duties as village marshal.

It was a long day. The hearing took almost six hours. F. H. Patterson, postmaster, was the leading witness for the prosecution. Many other witnesses were called. By the time all of the witnesses were called, it was evident that the facts in the case would never be clear. It seemed as though no two people saw exactly the same thing, and many of the so-called facts in the case would never be corroborated by evidence.

Lucy thought the day would never end. Her heart wrenched every time someone said something she did not think was in Charlie's favor. She wondered how there could have been so many people watching and yet all tell different stories. How could they possibly think that Charlie would kill a man unless it was self-defense? As she sat in that courtroom and listened to the prosecution's witnesses, Lucy wondered if Charlie was ever going to get to come home.

Finally, the hearing ended and the judge declared that bail for Charles R. Witwer would be set at four thousand dollars. A loud mummer went through the crowd. Lucy's shoulders slumped, and she felt faint when she heard the judge declare "four thousand dollars." Jim and Jacob were infuriated. They could feel Lucy beginning to waver in her seat and tried to prop her up as they glared at the judge. The three of them were immobilized by what they heard and could only stare in disbelief. That amount of money was an astronomical sum to the Witwer family. Jim and Jacob knew they would never be able to raise the bail money, which meant that Charlie would be sitting in that jail cell until the trial was over. As the initial shock subsided, they glanced over at Charlie. They saw him brace himself on the edge of the table and knew he was thinking the same thing they were. Charlie looked over his shoulder at them briefly, and they could see the pain in his eyes.

As the three of them listened to the final words of the judge, each of them had a hard time concentrating on what he was saying. Charlie was to be held over for a grand jury appearance, which was to take place on September 15, 1915, in Greene County. Meanwhile, he would continue to be held in the Greene County Jail, or until such time that bail was raised. September was almost six months away, six months that Charlie would be sitting in that jail—and then what! Lucy knew there was no way the family could raise four thousand dollars. She was not sure she had ever seen four hundred!

Once the court was adjourned, a low mummer swept through the crowd and then stopped suddenly. Everyone's eyes turned toward Jim, Lucy and Jacob as they rose from their seats. It was deadly quiet as the three of them left the courtroom. A few people nodded, but for the most part, there was little interaction between Charlie's family members and the spectators in the courtroom. All they wanted to do was to get back to the car as quickly as possible and get back to Jacksonville. It had become their safe haven.

The March 25 issue of the *Carrollton Patriot* reported, "It was a very large bond, and Charles Witwer might have a difficult time raising such a large amount." They also reported that there were few cases in the past that had generated such a complex situation for the justice system to try to sort out.

The events of the preliminary hearing was the main topic of discussion for many days in the restaurants, barber shops, general stores, saloons, and every other place that the townsfolk in Carrollton and Hillview congregated. Among those who took a strong interest in the case, the general thought was that the decision of the court to allow bond indicated that it was the court's opinion that there was evidence he had committed a crime but not murder to the fullest extent.

CHAPTER 44

Life in the County Jail

After the preliminary hearing, Charlie was taken back to the county jail, where, once again, he heard the clink of the cell door as it closed and locked behind him. Charlie knew that his family could not raise the bail money, so he would be sitting in that cell for another 179 days waiting for his appearance before the grand jury. He was a tough-minded person but spending 179 more days in that cell was almost beyond his comprehension. The only thing he had to look forward to were the visits from Lucy and the other members of his family.

As the last of winter turned into spring and spring blossomed into summer, Charlie's days passed routinely, one after the other. The monotony was almost more than he could bear. He would lie on the thin mattress on his cot and think of Lucy. He would close his eyes and remember how her eyes sparkled when she was happy. His heart would skip a beat as he remembered the happier times and dreamed of when he would once again be a free man.

The only contact he had with anyone, other than his attorneys, was when his meals were brought to him and when Lucy or a member of the family visited him. Sometimes Jim would bring Lucy for a visit so he too would visit with Charlie. It was not often that one of the other family members came to the jail for a visit, but he was elated when they did.

Charlie wanted to know everything that was going on with the family in Jacksonville. Sometimes they would tell him the same things over and over, but that was okay with Charlie. For a short time during the visit, he would feel he was a part of the family.

Charlie knew that the family did not have an abundant amount of money. Jim and Dick needed to work every day they could, and there was not much money to spare for train fare or gas. Visits with Charlie were stressful on Jacob and Nancy so they made very few trips to Carrollton. Charlie understood all of this, but he longed to see them and cherished the times they did come.

Occasionally, Sheriff Edwards or a deputy would put someone in one of the other cells, usually a fellow who had had too much to drink and was brought to the jail to sleep it off. He thought back to the sleepless nights he had spent in the Hillview jail listening to someone singing or yelling. It almost made Charlie chuckle to himself to think that he looked forward to having someone in another cell, even if he did sing or yell all night. It was a diversion from the boredom he felt each day and night.

Charlie knew that the events of that fateful day of March 6 had turned the lives of Lucy and his family upside down. He worried about them constantly. He knew he had filled many roles of responsibility in the family—he was a husband, a son, a brother, and brother in-law. He was the oldest male in the family, and they had always looked to him for support, both financially and emotionally. He had moved them all to Hillview, and now they had to start their lives over in Jacksonville. He had turned their lives upside down. He could hardly deal with the remorse he felt as he sat there day after day. Everyone in the family knew that Charlie worried about them, but they in turn worried about him.

Even though the Witwer family had a house to call their home, the days following their move to Jacksonville was a stressful time. They had no possessions other than what they had thrown together and carried on the train in suitcases and what had been packed in the Model T. Ernest, Jim, and Dick had packed so hurriedly that many things had to be left behind, and the Model T would hold just so much. Liz and Lucy had worked hard to make the house in Hillview a home and were sad to see so many things left behind. Once again, they were in a new city with few possessions, no friends, and this time, no means to support the family. Fortunately, Frank was able to help them during those first few weeks so they did not go hungry.

Jim and Dick were industrious fellows, though, and started looking for work immediately. They quickly found work as house painters and supported the family as best they could. One of the items that Dick made sure he packed when they left Hillview was his sewing machine repair case. He did not have any good memories about the time he spent in the reformatory as a teenager, but he knew that the skill of repairing sewing machines was a valuable one. He had always been able to make money wherever he lived using that skill. He knew women in Jacksonville would need their sewing machines repaired too. All he had to do was to get a couple of customers and the word of his skill would spread. So, between the painting jobs and the sewing machine repairs, the Witwer family began to feel a little bit of financial stability come back into their lives. At least they had food on the table! As usual, Nancy had her money jar. Jim and Dick knew she would be waiting on payday for most of their wages to be put into it.

Lucy was only twenty years old and felt the strain of the tumultuous months she had endured since her marriage to Charlie. During the twenty-six months she had been married, she had moved from her parents' home to live with Charlie's family; they had moved to Hillview with Charlie's brothers for Charlie to take the position of village marshal; she had given birth to a son and had buried him; she had been uprooted once again and moved to yet another unfamiliar town after the shooting; and now her husband had a murder charge hanging over his head and was facing a grand jury. How much more could she endure? She cried herself to sleep night after night until she thought she had no more tears left. Nevertheless, each morning she would rise to cook breakfast with Liz and be thankful that Charlie was safe.

Lucy had been happy when Charlie had taken the job as village marshal in Hillview. She did not like the traveling he did as a railroad detective and wanted him to be home more. Many days during those spring and summer months in Jacksonville, she stood scrubbing the pots and skillets, looking out the window with its cracked putty, wishing she could turn back the clock to the time that Charlie worked for the railroad. She would shake her head, as if that might make those thoughts go away, and busy herself with the next chore, trying to forget all that had happened. She knew she had to be strong for Charlie. She did not want to make his burden even heavier because she knew he worried about her and the rest of the family.

There was not a lot of extra money in the Witwer household. As often as she could, Nancy would give Lucy a few coins so she could hop the train and visit Charlie. Nancy seemed to know when Lucy was having a hard day coping and would slip her the coins. Sometimes Lucy would go alone, and sometimes one of the others would go with her. Occasionally, Jim was able to take her in the car. Lucy was always excited to see Charlie, but each time she left with overwhelming feelings of sorrow and frustration. On many occasions, she had heard Charlie and his brothers talk about the gangs who roamed the streets of Hillview and remembered the harassment and threats. She knew Charlie was a good man and was sure he had only acted in self-defense in the shooting of Clarence Deeds. She would never believe anything else.

As Charlie's days fell into the same pattern day after day, so did the days for the Witwer family. Jim and Dick found as much work as they could to support the family while Lucy and Liz took care of the house chores. They did not get out much but found enjoyment in trips to the grocery store or occasionally going downtown. Nancy helped when they would let her. Jacob was not a young man, so he spent most of his time sitting on the porch as the days turned warm.

The days, weeks and months passed slowly. Even on the sunniest days of summer, there was always a black cloud hanging over everyone's head with Charlie in the Carrollton jail. The days were not as tension-filled as they were in Hillview though. At least they did not get up every morning wondering what type of violence the day might bring. Everyone just wanted September 15 to hurry up and come so the grand jury would meet, but they also dreaded what would happen if Charlie was found guilty of murder.

CHAPTER 45

The Grand Jury

As the sun came up on September 15, 1915, it was just another day for most people, but not for Charlie or the Witwer family. This was the day everyone had been anxiously waiting for—the day Charlie would appear before the grand jury. They had been waiting almost six months.

No one in the Witwer family had gotten much sleep the night before. Everyone was up and ready to go long before it was time to leave to make the trip to Carrollton. Anxiety levels were running high!

They had decided that Nancy and Jacob would be more comfortable riding on the train, while Lucy, Liz, Dick, and Jim drove to Carrollton in the Model T. Their nerves were on edge, and there was hardly a word spoken as they picked at their breakfast. Jim drove Nancy and Jacob to the train station and then went back to the house to pick up the other three. Everyone was eager to get to Carrollton and to have the day over. They felt like they had been in a state of limbo these past months and hoped this was the day Charlie would be released from jail.

During the past months, there were times when Charlie hardly knew what day it was or what the date was. The daily routine rarely changed, and one day blended into another as time dragged by. Charlie knew what this day was, though. The morning started out just like any other morning, but Charlie knew that when the cell door opened, he was headed for the grand jury hearing. It was the day he had been waiting for, and, yet, almost dreaded.

Jacob and Nancy arrived in Carrollton and sat in the train station until Jim came to pick them up. It was not far to the courthouse, but Jim did not want them walking. Jim dropped Liz, Dick, and Lucy off at the courthouse and drove directly to the station to pick up Jacob and Nancy. He parked the car across the street from the courthouse when he returned. They found Liz, Lucy, and Dick standing quietly on the street corner in a tight huddle. They stayed in a tight group but with their heads held high as they walked to the courthouse, up the steps, and through the wide double doors into the hallway. They had made this trip before!

As they stood outside the courtroom waiting for the doors to open and watching the faces of other people who were milling around—many of whom had come from Hillview—the Witwers felt shunned by some but received a nod and slight smile from others. Some of the people were simply there as curious onlookers, while others had a strong interest in what was to take place behind those closed doors. No one knew how long they would be waiting, but Lucy was determined she was not leaving until she knew what was going to happen to her husband. No matter how strong everyone's interest was in the case, or if they were just curious onlookers, they all wondered the same thing. Would Charlie Witwer be a free man at the end of the day or would he be standing trial for murder?

When the doors of the courtroom opened, the Witwer family headed for the front row once again. They wanted to be as close to Charlie as they could, and they wanted him to see them as soon as he was brought into the courtroom. Lucy, Liz, and Nancy sat close to one another holding each other's hands. As Charlie was brought into the room, his gaze locked with Lucy's. They tried to give each other a reassuring smile, but the strain was evident on their faces. As his eyes slid over the rest of the family, they each smiled and nodded their heads.

As the morning proceeded, there were four witnesses that appeared and gave testimony: F. H. Patterson, H. H. Patterson, Clarence Turner, and Harry Newman. Each told his story as to what he thought had happened the night of the shooting. It was hard for the Witwer family to listen when things were said about Charlie that was not to his benefit. They knew Charlie, and they knew he would not kill someone unless he had no choice. As the verdict was called for, you could have heard a pin drop in the courtroom. No one moved to make the floors creak, and it seemed as though everyone was holding his or her breath.

As Charlie stood with his jaw clenched, eyes straight ahead, the foreman of the grand jury read: "Charles R. Witwer, in the manner and by the means aforesaid, and at the time and place aforesaid, unlawfully, willfully, felonious and of his malice aforethought did kill and murder the said Clarence Deeds."

Hearing those words, Charlie did not think he could take a breath. He felt as though there was an anvil on his chest, and his head pounded with the blood rushing through. He could hardly bring himself to turn around to look at Lucy and his family. He knew these past months had taken a toll on each of them. Jacob and Nancy seemed to have aged before his eyes, and Lucy seemed to have gotten thinner every time he saw her. Once he regained his composure, he turned to see them sitting like statues. He caught Lucy's eye and tried to give her a reassuring smile.

People jumped up from their seats, some shouting against the verdict and others for it. Lucy and the family sat glued to their seats. They could hardly believe what they were hearing. Once order was restored, based on that indictment, the judge announced that Charlie was to stand trial on September 20 for the shooting of Clarence Deeds.

Everyone in the family was devastated when they heard those words read, but none felt the pain as Lucy did. Her thoughts tumbled so rapidly in her mind she could hardly make sense of what had been said. Charlie was not to be a free man but would have to stand trial! She wondered how much more she could withstand. She burst into tears while Liz and Nancy tried to comfort her, but they too had tears streaming down their faces. Jacob, Dick, and Jim tried their best to contain their anger. Jim and Jacob took hold of Dick's arm to get a rein on him before he caused such a commotion that he was thrown in jail too. They did not need two Witwers sitting in jail! As Charlie was being led out of the courtroom, they could think of nothing but getting the women back to the car and away from the crowd.

As tough as the men were, they too had tears brimming over and trickling down their cheeks as they walked back to the Model T. Jim hurriedly took Jacob and Nancy back to the train station while Lucy, Liz, and Dick stood on the corner waiting for him to come back and pick them up. Lucy and Liz wore their large-brimmed straw hats and kept their heads down, not wanting to look at anyone.

As the family traveled back to Jacksonville, everyone was sad and sullen and had little to say. Even Dick, whose anger always reared its head, had no words to express his feelings. They had no choice but to return to Jacksonville and continue their daily lives until it was time to make another trip to Carrollton for the trial. They were so very thankful the trial had been set for September 20—only five more days. Lucy would not only be counting the days, but would be counting the hours! She, as well as the rest of the family, wanted the trial to be over as quickly as possible, but the dread of what the outcome might be lay heavily on the hearts of each one of them. They did not want to lose hope, though.

Chapter 46

The Trial Begins

The trial of Charles R. Witwer for the murder of Clarence Deeds began on Tuesday, September 20, 1915; approximately two years after Charlie had been named village marshal of Hillview. An altercation with several rowdies in a saloon was the catalyst for him being asked to be the village marshal, and an altercation with some of the same rowdies resulted in the death of one of them two years later.

Charlie had spent six months in his jail cell thinking back over all of the incidents that had occurred during his time as marshal and how he and his brothers had dealt with them. When he took the job, he had been sure he could make the town a safer place, but now he wasn't sure if he had made much progress. He wondered if anyone would be able to clean up Hillview until the town decided they wanted the streets free of violence. Rolling all of this around in his head as he paced back and forth in his cell day after day did nothing but cause him anguish.

Charlie spent the next three days going over the shooting incident with the two attorneys that had been appointed to defend him prior to the grand jury hearing—Judge Thomas Hinshaw of Carrollton and E. C. Knots of Carlinville. Sometimes only one attorney spent time with Charlie, and at other times, both of them questioned him repeatedly. Charlie was steadfast in what he told them: He shot Clarence Deeds only after being attacked by him. He did so only because none of the bystanders would come to his rescue and he feared for his life. He never wavered as they questioned him. To him, these were cold, hard facts. He told them every detail so that nothing important was forgotten.

When the attorneys left each day, Charlie replayed the conversations over and over in his head. Was he making them understand what had happened? Did they believe him? Did he forget to mention any little important detail? He was so exhausted at the end of each day, he felt like he had been doing hard labor from sunup to sundown. He was so exhausted that he slept soundly for a few hours each night.

For the rest of the world, when the sun came up on September 20, it was no different than any other day, but for Charlie and his family, it was one of the most important days in their lives. Lucy and Liz cooked breakfast as usual, but they hurried everyone to finish so they could get the dishes cleaned up. Lucy's only thought was to get to Carrollton as quickly as they could. Once again, Jim took Nancy and Jacob to the train station and then went back to the house to get Lucy, Liz, Dick, and Ernest. Ernest had come to Jacksonville the day before so he could attend the trial with the rest of the family.

The five of them loaded into the Model T and headed for Carrollton on the warm, fall day. Dick crowded into the backseat with Liz and Lucy, so it was a rather uncomfortable drive, but they were so engrossed in their thoughts they hardly noticed. Even though their thoughts were glum, they were glad the sun was shining and that it was warm so they did not have to bundle up.

One more time, they trudged up the courthouse steps with heavy hearts. They wanted to be in the front row once again so they could see Charlie, and he could see them. They wanted to hear every word that was said and wanted to watch the faces of the jury as testimonies were given. The minute the courtroom doors opened, they scurried in. Following them was a crowd of people that filled the courtroom. It was not often there was a murder trial going on, so many townspeople who had little interest in this particular case showed up just to watch. The morning train had been full of people from Hillview eager to see what the fate of Charles Witwer would be. There was not an empty seat to be found when the courtroom doors were closed.

A hush fell over the courtroom as Charlie was brought into the room. Charlie held his head high and walked with a sense of pride. Regardless of what the coroner's verdict had been or what the grand jury's verdict had been, he knew he had shot Clarence Deeds in self-defense, and when he had shot him, he had not intended to kill him.

Before sitting down, Charlie paused to look at Lucy and each one of his family members. He tried to smile at them before he took the empty seat between his two attorneys. He sat rigid in a wooden straight-back chair with his hands on his thighs.

A pool of one hundred jurors had been called for the two trials that were scheduled on the docket in Greene County that week. The jury selection for Charlie's trial began that morning, but by the end of the day when the court was recessed, there still was not a full jury selected. Everyone had been glued to their seats all day watching the process, except for during the brief lunch break.

You could almost feel the tension crackle in the air as the prospective jurors were interviewed. Late in the afternoon when the judge declared that court would be recessed until the following morning, you could hear a sigh ripple through the crowd. Everyone was exhausted. The Witwers were glad the day was over but wished there had been more progress. They now had to ride back to Jacksonville knowing they would have to make the same trip to Carrollton the next day. With jury selection progressing so slowly, they all wondered just how many more days they would be making the same trip.

The next morning, Nancy got up early and cooked breakfast for everyone. Nancy knew Lucy was exhausted just from the stress and would appreciate her help. When they had gotten home the night before, everyone was so tired and worn out that no one wanted to fix supper. As a result, no one had had much to eat.

As they sat around the kitchen table, Jacob told the rest of the family that he and Nancy would not be going back to the trial that morning. They both were up in years, and the trip was difficult for them. Sitting in the courtroom all day was even more difficult. Nancy told them she would cook supper so that when they got home that night, they would have a good meal. Once again, Lucy, Liz, Jim, Ernest, and Dick piled into the Model T for the trip to Carrollton.

As the jury selection was completed the second day of the trial, Charlie and his brothers were surprised to see that not one of those selected was from Hillview. Charlie was not able to discuss this with Jim, Dick, and Ernest, but he knew they were thinking the same thing that he was.

The four brothers had come to know just about everybody in Hillview, and they did not know any of the jurors. They did not know much about jury selection, but they whispered to each other that maybe this would be good for Charlie. They watched as Charlie's attorneys took every opportunity available to object to anyone from Hillview being on the jury.

To the relief of everyone, the jury was finally selected after hours of questioning prospective jurors. The jury panel for Charlie's trial was made up of the following individuals: George P. Williams, J. P. Henderson, and William Pour from Roodhouse; Joseph Van Meter, Henry Morrison, and Albert Lovel from Rockbridge; Thomas J. Grant and Frank Allen from White Hall; Joe Knight and Joe

Naber from Carrollton; Elmer Ashford from Wrights; and Frank Muntz from Rubicon.

CHAPTER 47

Witnesses Are Called

During the trial, thirty witnesses were subpoenaed for the prosecution but only ten were called to testify. There were only four witnesses for the defense. Charlie's attorneys chose not to call Charlie to testify on his own behalf. The examination of witnesses started on Thursday and lasted through Saturday. Each day the Witwer family made the trip to Carrollton, and each night they went back to Jacksonville. They dreaded making each trip, but they had no choice.

As the witnesses were called to give their testimonies, the witnesses who were present at the time of the shooting gave different accounts of what took place prior to the shooting, during the scuffle, and the shooting itself.

Most of the witnesses did agree that Isom Leonard, Clarence Deeds, and the other two young men standing in the street had been drinking and were shouting threats of bodily harm at Charlie just minutes before they approached him. Most witnesses also agreed that when Charlie attempted to arrest Isom Leonard, Clarence Deeds interfered, and that is when the altercation between Charlie and Clarence Deeds began.

It was a very long three days of testimony for the Witwer family. Their emotions were on a roller coaster. When they heard something in Charlie's favor, they would get their hopes up, and when something was said that could be detrimental, they would fall into a pit of despair. How could there be so many different accounts of what took place? Would the jurors believe that Clarence Deeds was shot in self-defense? Would this trial never end!

Even though there rarely was any emotion that showed on Charlie's face, he was on the same emotional roller coaster. His stomach clenched and he clasped his hands together to keep them steady. Occasionally, you could see his cheeks burn, and his family knew that his anger was rising to the surface. Charlie knew that any type of outburst from him would not be beneficial, so he continued to stare directly at each witness with a calm outward appearance. Occasionally one of Charlie's attorneys would put a hand on his shoulder.

The *Carrollton Patriot* reported that the most important evidence on the part of the defense related to a plot concocted before the day of the shooting. Witnesses testified that they had heard Clarence Deeds and other gang members threaten "to get rid of Village Marshal Charlie Witwer and Mayor Coates, one way or the other."

By the time the court was adjourned on Saturday, all of the witnesses had been called for both the prosecution and the defense. Once again, Charlie was taken back to his jail, and the Witwer family headed back to Jacksonville. By this time, each one of them knew every bend and pothole in the road.

Court was recessed until Monday morning. Sunday was a very long day in the Witwer household. Everyone tried to keep busy, but it was hard to think about anything except for what Monday was going to bring. Jim and Dick had not worked for several days, which put a financial strain on the family. So many things to worry about! They wanted this trial to be over with for more than one reason.

Each evening when they got home from Carrollton during that week, Nancy had a hot meal ready for them. By the time they drove back to Jacksonville at the end of the day, they were ready for a good meal. Sometimes it was difficult to eat after a tension-filled day, particularly for Lucy. Lucy knew she had to eat just to keep going. She was so thankful to have Nancy in the household and taking on the responsibility of cooking and the household chores. Most days, Nancy would pack something for them to eat during the noon break since they did not have a lot of money to spend at the restaurant. Lucy and Liz did not like going to a restaurant anyway. They always felt like people were staring at them and gossiping about the trial. Lucy and Jim spent each evening trying to tell Jacob and Nancy what had transpired that day during the trial.

Monday, September 26, 1915, was once again just another day in the lives of most people. And, for the Witwer family, even the days they made the trek to Carrollton had fallen into a pattern. Nancy cooked breakfast again that morning. After eating, Jim, Dick, Lucy, and Liz piled into the Model T, while Nancy and Jacob stood on the porch watching them go. Ernest had gone back to his home in New Berlin on Sunday but promised to be back on Tuesday. Nancy and Jacob stood on the porch early that Monday morning wondering how many more days the trial would go on. The days were long for them as they waited for the return of their family each night. Nancy tried to keep busy cleaning the house and cooking a hot meal but many times found herself staring into space paralyzed with the thought of what might happen to her firstborn son. Jacob would put his jacket on and walk around the yard until his legs were almost too tired to walk up the front porch steps to get back into the house. Little was said between the two of them as all of the words had already been spoken.

Lucy, Liz, Jim, and Dick took their usual seats that Monday morning. There was still a large crowd of people in the courtroom, but it had thinned out somewhat. This was the sixth day of the trial, so some people had lost interest in what was happening. Only those individuals that were truly interested in the outcome of the trial of Charles Witwer came back each day as the trial progressed.

The closing arguments took the entire day on Monday, one week after the trial had started. The prosecuting attorney claimed that Charles Witwer's actions were not within the law, nor were they taken in the line of his duty as a village marshal. He told the jury that Charlie had a weapon hidden in his pocket rather than carrying it in plain sight in a holster, as a law officer should. He stated that putting this weapon in his pocket, and not in a visible place, showed that his actions were with malice of forethought.

The prosecuting attorney also attempted to convince the jury that the defendant harbored so much hostility toward Deeds and Leonard, who Witwer believed were the ringleaders of the troublemakers, that he did not hesitate to pull the weapon from his pocket and use it to kill Deeds. He reminded the jury that neither Deeds nor Leonard displayed weapons of any kind as they approached the defendant, so the defendant's actions were entirely too radical for the situation. The prosecuting attorney acknowledged that even though there might have been some harsh words and a struggle between Deeds and the defendant, these circumstances did not justify the use of a weapon that could inflict death on an individual. The jury was asked to find the defendant "guilty of premeditated murder."

When Lucy heard this, she could hardly keep from jumping up and yelling at the prosecuting attorney and the jury. They just could not find her husband guilty of premeditated murder! As he felt Lucy start to move, Jim put his arm around her shoulders to try to comfort her, although he felt the same way. Jim was afraid that Dick might jump up at any time and shout something, but Dick did not move a muscle.

The family sat and watched, along with the other spectators, as the defense counsel argued that the defendant, Charles Witwer, attempted to defend himself first with his cane. When the cane broke, he had no other means of protecting himself when he was approached by Leonard and attacked by Deeds. The defense counsel reminded the jury that the defendant had called for help from the people on the street since he was outnumbered, and nobody attempted to help him. Everyone simply remained as bystanders and watched as the scuffle took place. He also told the jury that the defendant struggled loose from his attacker once and tried to flee from the situation. However, Deeds once again attacked him. As the defendant removed the gun from his pocket and shot his attacker, he was only doing so in self-defense and within the realm of an officer of the law. The defense attorney reminded the jury of the numerous threats that had been made on the defendant's life and on the life of the mayor.

Defense counsel tried to impress upon the jury that not only was Charles Witwer on trial, but so was the law enforcement system in Hillview. If the defendant was convicted, it would send a message that no law enforcement officer would have the right to do his duty or to protect himself if he felt that his life was being threatened, and that those who roamed the streets causing trouble would only become bolder in their disregard for the law. Defense counsel also asked the jury to consider the fact that the first thing the defendant did immediately after the shooting was to call Sheriff Edwards. Defense counsel reminded the jury that Mayor Coates thought the threats against the defendant and himself were so serious that he and his family left town that very night.

Charlie watched every move that was made during the closing arguments and listened to every word. He made eye contact with every juror, never showing any emotion. He was a stoic person by nature. Nothing was said by any witness or any attorney that caused him to change his demeanor. He sat rigidly in his straight-back chair every day as he watched what was taking place in the courtroom. During these closing arguments, his behavior was no different. Occasionally, one of his attorneys would whisper something to him, and he would simply nod his head in return.

This jury had his life in their hands, and Charlie knew it! To all those who were watching, he may have looked calm, but they could not begin to imagine what he was feeling. His heart was racing, and his head was pounding. He tried to take deep breaths to calm himself down. Several times, he had to clasp his hands together to keep them from shaking.

CHAPTER 48

The Verdict

Once the prosecuting attorneys and the defense attorneys completed their closing arguments and rested their cases late in the afternoon, the judge made the decision to *not* adjourn the court until the next day. He advised them that court would resume at 7:30 p.m. This came as quite a surprise to everyone in the courtroom. It had already been a very long day, but it was going to get even longer. Lucy did not know whether to be happy that maybe it would all be over that night or if she wanted to prolong the jury's verdict until the next day. The judge had spoken, though, and they had no choice but to return at 7:30 p.m.

The Witwer family scurried across the street to the restaurant to see if they could get something to eat. They had not come prepared to stay into the evening hours. They had no idea what the judge had in mind or what time they would be leaving the courtroom that night. They knew Jacob and Nancy would be very worried when they did not come home in the early evening hours as they had every other day, but there was no way to get a message to them.

At 7:30 when the court was resumed, the Witwer family sat in their usual places. These benches seemed to get harder every time they sat down on them. You could see the weariness and strain on their faces. Very few people had returned for the evening session. Charlie was once again brought in to take his place in front of the judge and jury. He looked as weary as the rest of them but continued to hold his head high. He never failed to turn to look at his family, give them a quick smile, and nod his head.

As soon as Judge Jones sat down, he looked at Charlie for several seconds and then turned to the jury and said, "The court instructs the jurors that even though you may believe from the evidence that the defendant did unlawfully strike Clarence Deeds with a cane at the time of the altercation, if Deeds was in Patterson's store cursing and threatening the defendant, still if you further believe from the evidence that after striking such a blow or blows, the defendant in good faith withdrew or sought to withdraw from further combat, then said Deeds had no lawful right to pursue the defendant and grapple with or throw him down or bite or chew on his ear or otherwise do or attempt to do him bodily harm and injury. And, if you further believe from the evidence that after the defendant did strike such blows with his cane, he did in good faith withdraw from further difficulty with said Deeds, and that said Deeds did pursue the defendant and grapple with him and thereby cause the defendant in good faith to believe as a reasonable prudent and peaceful man that he was in danger of losing his own life or receiving serious bodily injury, then the defendant had the lawful right to defend himself, even to the taking of a life of said Deeds, then you must find the defendant *not guilty*.

The court instructs the jury that if you believe from the evidence, beyond a reasonable doubt, that the defendant Charles Witwer assaulted the deceased, Clarence Deeds, with a deadly weapon, after which the said Witwer and the said Deeds clenched and engaged in a struggle, and that the said Witwer did not in good faith decline further combat before he fired the fatal shot, and that the said fatal shot was fired by the said Witwer with malice aforethought, and the defendant Witwer would be *guilty* of murder and you should so find by your verdict of murder."

The jurors were sent into the jury room for deliberation at about 8:00 p.m. Everyone wondered how long they would be deliberating. The first ballot rendered by the jury came out within a short time, which surprised most of those in the courtroom. Regardless of how much Lucy and the rest of the family wanted this trial to be over, were they ready to hear a verdict? When they heard that the vote was eight for the acquittal of the defendant and four for conviction they did not know what to think. They each were in a state of confusion. Now what was going to happen?

The judge was quick to make a decision and sent the jurors back into the jury room to deliberate once again. It appeared that the judge was not going to let this trial go on for another day. As tired as the Witwer family was, they were glad the judge had made this decision. At this point, they were beyond tired! All they could think of was that there were more votes for an acquittal than for a conviction.

A second ballot was taken soon after the jury returned to the jury room. The jury returned to the courtroom, and the ballot was taken to the judge. This time the vote was eleven to one in favor of the defendant. Relief washed over the Witwer family, and they hardly felt their tiredness. They were elated! Now what was going to happen?

The judge sat quietly for a few minutes, which seemed like hours to Lucy. He looked at the jury and once again told them to return to the jury room. This time the evidence was deliberated for almost two hours.

As the minutes ticked by, the weary Witwer family sat solemnly in the courtroom. They had spent every day on those hard benches and heard every word that was said during the trial. This was the sixth day they had driven to Carrollton. Each evening on the previous days, when they had driven back to Jacksonville, they never knew what the next day was going to bring and wondered how many days the trial would go on. They were now convinced the judge was determined that this trial was going to be over that very night. Why else would he be sending the jury back to their room for more deliberation? They were all very weary, and they knew that Charlie, the jurors, the judge, and everyone else in the courtroom had to be weary also.

As the minutes ticked by, it became more and more difficult to sit and wait, and yet there was nothing else to do. They had nowhere to go. Lucy's thoughts were with Charlie. If only she could go and sit by him, she would feel so much better. She saw Liz leaning her head against Dick's shoulder, and saw Jim pacing in the back of the courtroom. She knew Jim was so nervous that he could not sit still, although he, too, was thoroughly worn out as the rest of them were. Oh, would this never end?

At 11:00 p.m., the jury returned to the courtroom. They too looked tired and bleary-eyed as they shuffled back to their seats, but there was no emotion playing on their faces. They looked directly at the judge as they took their seats.

As the judge rapped his gavel, Jim scurried back to sit by Lucy and grabbed her hand. He squeezed it so hard Lucy thought it would break. There was yet to be another verdict read. What would it be this time? Guilty or not guilty? Or, would the jury have been able to come to a consensus? If not, what would the judge do? All of these thoughts scrambled through everyone's minds.

Once again, there was not a sound to be heard. For the Witwer family and Charlie, there did not seem to be enough air in the room to breathe. Or were they just holding their breath?

The jury foreman stood and advised the judge that they had come to a consensus. He slowly handed a folded piece of paper to the bailiff, who in turn presented it to Judge Jones. As he opened the folded paper, the judge hesitated briefly, looked up at those in the courtroom and then nodded to the jury. He stared straight at Charles R.

Witwer, the defendant, and asked him to rise. No one could even guess what was on that paper by watching the judge.

Charlie stood, his eyes never wavering from the judge. Judge Jones said in a clear voice, "By a unanimous vote of the jury, the court finds defendant Charles R. Witwer *not guilty*. Mr. Witwer, you are a free man."

Charlie never moved, but whatever tiredness Lucy, Jim, Liz, and Dick were feeling left immediately. *Not guilty*—those words were music to their ears! They jumped up from their seats as joy washed over them. They jumped up and down and started hugging each other while crying tears of joy. They had shed so many tears of sorrow in the past months that these were welcome tears. Charlie finally turned to look at them over his shoulder, and they had never seen him with such a big grin on his face.

There were a few people left in the courtroom, some who were outraged by the jury's verdict. These were presumed to be friends or family members of Clarence Deeds. Once Sheriff Edwards had received information that the judge seemed to be determined to get the jury to agree on a verdict that night, he had called in a couple of his deputies and placed them in the back of the courtroom. He did not want any violence when the verdict was read, regardless of whether it was a guilty or not guilty verdict. A couple of individuals were quickly ushered out of the courtroom when the verdict was read, when it looked like they might cause trouble but nothing serious took place. Sheriff Edwards knew that the last train for Hillview had passed through earlier in the evening, so most of those from Hillview had already left. He even wondered if Judge Jones considered this when he recessed the court in the late afternoon only to resume it at 7:30 p.m.

When Charlie first heard those words—not guilty—he was too stunned to react, but it did not take long for him to recover. Hearing "Mr. Witwer, you are a free man" jolted him so much that he felt like he had just been hit by a bolt of electricity. He was going to be a free man after six months of sitting in a jail cell wondering what his fate would be!

Charlie's attorneys were watching Charlie as he turned and smiled at his wife and family. They had not seen him smile in all of the hours they had spent with him before the trial. As Charlie turned to them and stuck his hand out, they could see the tension releasing from his shoulders and from his face. As they all shook hands, Charlie said, "Thank ya very much. I 'preciate what ya did fer me." Charlie turned back to look at the jury. Those men and women had held his fate in their hands. He would be forever grateful for the verdict they finally had rendered.

The judge ordered the courtroom to be cleared, and the deputy sheriffs escorted Charles R. Witwer, a free man, through the side door. All Charlie wanted to do was to find Lucy and the rest of his family. As Charlie stepped out into the cool night air, Sheriff Edwards approached him with a big smile on his face.

"Congratulations, Charlie. You got a fair trial and a fair verdict. I know your family will be waiting for you, but I need you to come to the jail with me. I've asked a deputy to be with your family so don't worry about them. This'll only take a few minutes."

Charlie did not know why Sheriff Edwards was taking him to the jail. He had spent enough time there and had no desire to see the inside of it again. He did not question, though, but simply walked with the sheriff and the deputy. Walking into the jail this time did not bring on the anxiety that it had all of the other times he had walked through those doors during those past months. Once inside, Sheriff Edwards unlocked a drawer in his desk and pulled out a brown paper bag. He handed it to Charlie as Charlie looked at him quizzically.

"I told you that when this was over I would return your pistol to you. It's not loaded. I think you are a good lawman, and you should consider making a career in law enforcement."

Charlie took a long look at the pistol and then at Sheriff Edwards. "My law enforcement days 're over, but I 'preciate yer kind words. Right now, all I want ta do is be with my family."

As the deputy walked with Charlie from the jail to the Model T where the family was standing, Dick and Jim were still slapping each other on the back as they both talked at the same time. Liz kept grabbing Lucy and hugging her. As Lucy stood waiting for Charlie, she never took her eyes off the street that led to the jail. She did not know why the sheriff took Charlie back to the jail and was anxious to see him. When she finally saw Charlie coming down the street, her weariness rolled away. She ran and threw her arms around his neck and sobbed as the tension flowed out of her body. Liz, Dick, and Jim stood back until they could not stand it any longer. They all ran up to Charlie and Lucy and threw their arms around both of them. There was no happier family in the country at that moment.

They finally piled into the Model T anxious to head for home. Their home would now be complete—brother Charlie would be there with them. Everyone was jubilant as they drove back to Jacksonville, even though it was very late and they were very tired. When they arrived at the family home, even though it was after midnight, Jacob and Nancy came rushing to the door. They had been waiting anxiously wondering what had happened when the family did not show up for supper at the end of the day. The only thing they could imagine was that there was car trouble.

When Jacob and Nancy heard the sound of a car coming up the street, they opened the door to peer out. As the car pulled into the driveway and Nancy saw Charlie jump out of the Model T, she ran down the sidewalk hollering, "Thank God!" She did not care if the whole neighborhood heard her or saw her nightgown flapping in the wind. Jacob was quick to follow and threw his arms around both Nancy and Charlie. All they knew right then was that Charlie was at home, so this nightmare must be over.

As the family made their way into the house, everyone was chattering all at once. Nancy and Jacob had a hundred questions they wanted answered. After giving them a quick rundown of what had happened that day, with a promise to talk about it more in the morning, Charlie announced that he was tired and everyone else was too. It was time to go to bed! Tomorrow would be another day to answer questions and to look over his new home. All he wanted to do was sleep in a bed where there were no bars surrounding him or a locked door that he could not open. He wanted to wake up to the smell of biscuits and gravy with Lucy at his side. In his jail cell, "tomorrow" did not have much significance, but now it took on a new meaning.

Tomorrow he would become acquainted with his new home.

Tomorrow he would enjoy being with Lucy and his family.

Tomorrow he would get to know his neighbors.

Tomorrow he would get in touch with his other two brothers, Frank and Ernest.

Tomorrow he would explore his new city of residence.

Tomorrow, tomorrow, tomorrow!

For six months, his tomorrows were bleak. Thinking about all of the tomorrows as a free man was exhilarating!

Witwer Pit Stop, Mound Avenue, Jacksonville, Illinois

CHAPTER 49

Starting Over

As the days turned into weeks and the weeks into months, life took on a sense of being "normal," which was just fine with each member of the Witwer family. They had had enough change, heartache, stress, and tension in the previous two years to last a lifetime. They would never again want anything but a "normal" day. They felt as though their lives had been torn apart and put into a holding pattern since the shooting had occurred and the flight to Jacksonville had taken place. For six months, they wondered what was going to be the fate of Charlie and what was going to happen to the family if he was convicted. Now they could begin to live their lives again and look forward to the future. They wanted nothing more than to get on with their lives and forget the past two years.

Charles R. Witwer was a free man, but this was a life-changing episode in the life of Charlie as well as for the rest of his family. When the trial was over, those two years in Charlie's life were not ones that he wanted to discuss.

Charlie rarely ventured out of the city of Jacksonville, even when Lucy traveled on the train to Mexico, Missouri, to see her family. Charlie never again worked in any type of law enforcement, nor did he have any desire to.

Every year on March 6, that fateful day of the shooting, Lucy would remember what happened but she and Charlie did not discuss it. It was a closed book to

Charlie, never to be opened again. March 6 and the days to follow were a nightmare. That nightmare ended September 20, 1915, and it was one he did not want to relive. Once he explained what had taken place during the trial to his parents and to Frank and Ernest, he never let anyone engage him in any conversation about it.

The End

Epilogue

It did not take Charlie long to begin looking for work once he was declared a free man and living with his family in Jacksonville. He was the oldest son, and it was still his responsibility to see that his family was taken care of. He quickly found work as a house painter and carpenter and spent most of his life involved in these trades. Of course, he went back to hunting and trapping in his spare time. Within a couple of years, he and Lucy began raising their family. Charlie and Lucy had two daughters, Goldie and Elnora (the mother of the author of this book). Charlie opened one of the first gas stations in Jacksonville, Illinois, in about 1920. It was located on the corner of College and Grand Avenue. There was a small apartment above the gas station where Charlie, Lucy, and their daughters lived for a short period of time. The family then moved to a small house that Charlie built. This house was a small bungalow and was located about a block from the gas station.

Just to the east of Charlie's gas station was a motel with three cabins, which were rented out to those who were traveling through Jacksonville. Charlie and Lucy ran the gas station and the motel for about seven or eight years. Those years were very prosperous for Charlie and Lucy, but that prosperity was not to last. In 1929, when Ayers Bank closed in Jacksonville and the Great Depression swept the nation, the Witwer family lost everything. They never recovered from this financial disaster and spent the rest of their life on the edge of poverty. Charlie always worked, though, and did his best to provide for his family.

During the first several years after the depression began, Charlie fell back on his house painting and carpentry skills and made a meager living. He continued hunting and trapping, which always gave him great joy. He loved the solitude of being in the woods. These were lean years for

Charlie and his family, as they were for many others in the United States.

Charlie eventually accumulated enough resources to build a small, one-room house, which had outdoor plumbing with an indoor well pump at the kitchen sink. This house was located at 108 Fairview. By this time, both of his daughters were married and starting families of their own.

Charlie never learned to drive a car. Lucy figured that if they were going to have a car, she was going to have to learn to drive, so she did. She drove Charlie around Jacksonville, when he chose not to walk. If someone recognized Lucy coming down the street in the car, he or she tried to get out of her way; she was notorious for driving down the middle of the streets in Jacksonville. Charlie chose to walk on many of his outings to the downtown area, which probably contributed to his good health, as he grew older.

In 1935, when Charlie was fifty-three years old and Lucy was forty, they took on the task of raising a grandson who was not yet a year old (the author of this book). This was certainly not something they had anticipated, but they never shirked from the responsibility. Charlie shared his love of hunting and trapping with this grandson. Lucy did her best to once again take on the role of being a mother.

Charlie died on March 28, 1969, at the age of eighty-seven in Jacksonville, Illinois. Lucy continued to live in the small house on Fairview until she died on March 31, 1977, at the age of eighty-one.

Jim Witwer

Jim Witwer married Stella Abernathy in 1920. One child was born out of this union. After divorcing Stella, Jim married Emily Adeline Stice (Addie) on June 14, 1921, and they had five children: Mr. Joy Witwer, Ruby Jane Witwer, Harley Davidson Witwer, Lloyd James Witwer, Jack James

Witwer, and Norma "June" Witwer. Jim was a house painter in Jacksonville and never lost his love for hunting and trapping. He moved to Winchester, Illinois, about fifteen miles west of Jacksonville, for a few years and then moved back to Jacksonville. Addie died in 1956 at the age sixty. Jim died April 18, 1978, at the age of ninety-three.

Dick Witwer

Dick Witwer always seemed to find trouble wherever he went. He had several skirmishes with the law after moving to Jacksonville and served time in prison for trying to break a friend out of jail. When he moved to Jacksonville with the rest of the Witwer family in 1915, he lived with them for a short while. He then moved to another residence in Jacksonville with his wife, Liz. Dick and Liz had ten children. He died on June 14, 1960, in Jacksonville, Illinois, at the age of sixty-eight from liver failure.

Ernest Witwer

Ernest Witwer got his wish and married Bertha Milby from New Berlin, Illinois. His lifelong dream of being involved in farming came to fruition when he moved to New Berlin and married Bertha, who was from a farming family. He and Bertha then moved to Scott County, Illinois, west of Winchester. This is where he raised his two sons, Jacob "Lee" and Ernest "Elmer" Witwer. Ernest died on September 15, 1963, at the age of seventy-seven in Winchester, Illinois.

Jacob and Nancy Witwer

Jacob and Nancy Witwer continued to live in the house on Lafayette Street in Jacksonville, Illinois, where Jacob died on June 24, 1920, at the age of eighty-seven. When her husband died, Nancy moved to California with her daughter, Rose. Nancy died on March 24, 1937, at the age of eighty-one in San Bernardino, California.

Sheriff Jesse Edwards

Sheriff Jesse Edwards, who played an important role in protecting and supporting Charlie Witwer and the Witwer family, continued as sheriff of Greene County, Illinois. His term ended in December of 1918. He mysteriously disappeared from Greene County on June 15, 1919. He was eventually located in Nobles County, Minnesota, where he was holding the position of sheriff.

On March 6, 1930, at age forty-eight, Jesse Edwards, who then farmed property north of Greenfield, Illinois, died at Our Savior's Hospital in Jacksonville, Illinois, following an undisclosed illness of about three days. (March 6 was the same day that Charlie Witwer shot Clarence Deeds.)

Mayor Lee Coates

Mayor Lee Coates, who was a full-time telegraph operator employed by the railroad as well as the mayor of Hillview, continued to live in Hillview and retired from the railroad after fifty-five years of service.

The Village

The small village of Hillview would forever remain divided on whether Village Marshal Charles R. Witwer acted in self-defense while performing his duties as a village marshal when he fatally shot Clarence Deeds after being assaulted by him, or whether their village marshal did so maliciously and was not performing his duties as village marshal

Clarence Deeds was remembered as not being a bad individual but just as a person that hung around with bad company and who drank too much, which many times led to trouble. Sometime after the shooting, Isom Leonard departed from the Hillview area.

Hillview, Illinois—Then and Now

Hillview continued to have problems with gangs on the streets. Finding someone to take over the law enforcement for the village was not an easy task. After several years, the McClay Orchards closed down, railroad passenger service was discontinued, businesses began to close, and the Illinois River flooded the town several times. At one time Hillview was considered one of the fastest growing communities in Illinois, but now it is just like so many other small towns—vacant lots, empty buildings, and abandoned houses.

At one time, on Saturday nights, the streets of Hillview were crowded. If people wanted a good parking space, they would have to take their car to the downtown area in the early afternoon to make sure they had a choice spot that evening. Now, there is no business sector to visit. Young people have a hard time believing that at one time Hillview was a thriving little community with promise of a bright future.

Hillview and the surrounding area have survived at least two devastating tornadoes in the area, in which several people were killed. The flood of 1993 caused the levy to break in two places. This almost wiped the village off the map, but there are always those who return to their homestead, no matter what happens.

Hillview remains on the map today with a population of less than two hundred. Even so, those who make Hillview their home are proud of their community.